THE FREE TRADE
PROPOSALS

THE
FREE TRADE
PROPOSALS

Edited by

G. D. N. WORSWICK
Fellow of Magdalen College, Oxford

OXFORD
BASIL BLACKWELL
1960

PART I first printed in the *Bulletin* of the Oxford University Institute of Statistics February 1957, Volume 19, No. 1.

PRINTED IN GREAT BRITAIN BY
COMPTON PRINTING WORKS LTD., LONDON
AND BOUND BY THE KEMP HALL BINDERY, OXFORD

PREFACE

In February 1957 the *Bulletin* of the Oxford University Institute of Statistics published a *Symposium* on the European Free Trade Area proposals. Mr. J. Black was invited to write an introductory article bringing together such readily available statistics as might provide a background against which the problems raised could be put into perspective. His article was then circulated to a number of leading economists who were asked to comment on it and to discuss any specific aspects of the proposals which seemed to them of especial importance. Part I of this book consists of the original *Symposium*, which has been out of print for some time. Part II is, with the exception of one chapter, entirely new material. Mr. Black has brought the statistical material up to date, and my own chapter summarises the main developments in the European Economic Community and the course of the negotiations for a European Free Trade Area up to the point of breakdown at the end of 1958. It seemed worth while in the light of this breakdown to ask the contributors to the original *Symposium* whether they wished to add any further comments. Sir Roy Harrod, Mr. Balogh and Professor Johnson have done so, and in addition I welcome a contribution from Mr. Day who did not write in the original *Symposium*. Professor Johnson's estimate of 'The Gains from Freer trade with Europe' was first published in *The Manchester School* in September 1958, and I am grateful to the Editor of that journal for permission to reprint it here. A word should be said about the time factor. Part I of the book was written at the end of 1956 and it is reproduced here exactly in its original form. The introductory chapters in the second part were written in early 1959 and the further contributions in the early summer of 1959, by which time it appeared that some form of free trade association of the 'Outer Seven' would probably be formed. These proposals are mentioned in this book but we have not attempted to go into them in any detail.

I should like to thank the Institute of Statistics for permission to use the *Symposium* material for this book, and to thank Miss B. M. Gisborne for typing successive drafts of a good many of the chapters.

G.D.N.W.

CONTENTS

vii

THE FREE TRADE
PROPOSALS

PART I

A SYMPOSIUM

THE IMPLICATIONS OF THE PROPOSED EUROPEAN FREE TRADE AREA

By J. BLACK

The purpose of this article is to provide some of the facts relevant to the implications for Great Britain of the proposed European Free Trade Area. The proposal under discussion is that the six 'Schumann Plan' countries, which already belong to the European Coal and Steel Community and operate a 'Common Market' for these products, should gradually over the next 12 to 15 years abolish tariffs on all trade among themselves, and have a common tariff against the goods of non-members. This plan would have the effect of confronting other countries, including Great Britain, with a choice between entering the Customs Union, making some form of special arrangement with it, or having their goods put at a disadvantage, relatively to the goods of any member, in selling to other members of the common market. The British Government has declared itself in favour of the second alternative, and at present favours the setting up of a ' Free Trade Area ' between the countries belonging to the customs union and Britain, by which Britain would gradually abolish tariffs on imports of non-agricultural goods from the customs union countries, which would do the same in return, but would retain her present tariff structure as regards trade with non-members, so that Britain's present preferential arrangements, which favour trade with the Commonwealth countries, could be retained.

Although the British Government is at present in favour of excluding agricultural commodities from the scope of the free trade area, it remains to

be seen whether this will prove acceptable either to the other members, or
to the members of the General Agreement on Tariffs and Trade. However,
as Britain is not the only country whose agriculturalists are likely to jib at
free trade it seems realistic to discuss the proposals on the assumption that
the British Government's proposals will—in some form and for some
consideration—be accepted.

It is uncertain, if the customs union and associated free trade area are
set up, how many countries would wish to join such a system, whether as
full members of the customs union, or by arrangements similar to Britain's.
Thus in considering the advantages and disadvantages, we cannot be certain
what the size of the new group would be; all the information given below is
therefore related to two possibilities, which may perhaps be regarded as the
limits of what could happen. The smallest possible group of members
would be the six Schumann Plan countries, which at present form the
European Coal and Steel Community; *i.e.* France, Western Germany,
Italy, the Netherlands, Belgium and Luxembourg. A second possibility
would be these plus Great Britain; but even if Britain did not join some other
European countries, particularly Austria, Switzerland and Denmark, might
well join, and if Britain did join then other countries would be encouraged
to do so, notably Norway and Sweden. Thus we take as the maximum
possible group, for purposes of argument, the whole of the European
membership of the O.E.E.C., plus Finland, but excluding Turkey. Some
members of the group thus defined might well feel unable to join, *e.g.* Greece
or Portugal, but their share in O.E.E.C. trade and production is small.
Though non-European countries might be invited to join, the prospects of
their doing so appear to be small.

The theoretical arguments in favour of the new common market all rely
on various economies it would make possible. These arise from three main
causes; the first is the possibility of increased productive efficiency in cases
where the existing national markets do not allow of production on the optimum scale, or where this would be possible within national markets only at
the cost of a degree of standardisation unacceptable to consumers. The
second is a greater utilisation of differences in comparative costs, by having
greater international specialisation, and locating production of each type of
good where it is most economical, though here the proposed exclusion of
agricultural products would remove one of the greatest potential sources of
benefit. The third is the effect of increased competition in stimulating
greater efficiency on the part of management and labour; here the existence
of tariffs may not be the most important source of restrictionism. Some of
the main arguments against Britain joining a European Free Trade Area are
given below; but before going on to these let us consider some of the facts
relevant to the arguments in favour of the scheme.

To develop an adequate factual background to all these arguments would
necessitate a series of detailed studies of particular industries and an attempt
to forecast in which of the ways mentioned above a greater measure of

freedom of trade would affect them, given the human and natural resources involved, their forms of organisation, etc. Such specialist studies cannot be improvised, so we must perforce be content with certain macro-economic information concerning both the size of the proposed European market, and the present trade in various commodity groups. While it cannot be assumed that the benefits of freer trade within any area increase in direct proportion to its size, by any given measure, it would appear reasonable to suppose that, for some industries at least, the benefits are an increasing function of the size of the new European market, and to compare it with the existing industrial giants, the U.S.A. and the U.S.S.R.

The total population of the 'Schumann Plan' Countries is 161 million: that of Britain is 51 million, and that of the rest of Western Europe a further 51 million (including Denmark, Norway, Sweden and Finland, with 19 million between them, and Austria, Eire, Greece, Iceland, Portugal and Switzerland with $31\frac{1}{2}$ million between them). Thus if Britain or the other Western European Countries joined, the population of the Free Trade Area would be 212 million, or if both joined, 263 million. This compares with 166 million in the U.S.A. and 215 million in the U.S.S.R. Since agricultural products are excluded from the proposals, it is also interesting to compare the labour force in Mining and Manufacturing, in the various countries. Thus in Britain, in 1951, of a total force of 23.2 million, 9.5 million or 41 per cent were in these occupations,[1] whereas in the Schumann Plan Countries, of a total labour force of 69.5 million, 21.3 million or 30.7 per cent worked in mining or manufacturing. In the rest of Western Europe, of a total labour force of 18.6 million, 4.9 million or 26.5 per cent worked in these groups. Thus if all the Western European countries were to join a Free Trade Area, it would contain a total labour force of over 111 million with 35.7 million or 32 per cent in mining and manufacturing, and Britain would have access to a market containing 4.8 times her own total labour force, and $3\frac{3}{4}$ times her labour force employed in mining and manufacturing. This compares with 60 million total labour force, of whom 17.1 million, or 28.5 per cent worked in mining or manufacturing in the United States in 1951.

Not all of the countries involved are equally rich; the size of the market they offer is governed by their total national incomes. Their Gross National Products may be compared (using official exchange rates); in 1954 Britain's G.N.P. was £17,900 mn., the total G.N.P. of the Schumann Plan Countries were £40,840 mn., and those for the rest of Western Europe £9,800 mn.; thus the combined G.N.P.'s of the Free Trade Area, if Britain joined, would be £68$\frac{1}{2}$ billion or nearly four times that of Britain alone. The United States G.N.P. in 1954 was £129 billion, or much larger than the largest possible European market—though it is hoped that greater co-operation between the European countries would enable them to increase the rate of growth of their total production.

[1] In 1955, of a total working force of 23,912,000, 10,068,000 or 42 per cent were in Mining and Quarrying and Manufacturing.

TABLE I

Working Population in Mining and Manufacturing

Note. The totals for groups of countries are figures for different dates, and can thus be used to indicate orders of magnitude only. Figures in '000s.

Area	Date of Census Data	Total Econ. Active pop.	Mining & Quar- rying	Manu- facturing	Man. & M. & Q.	Percent- age of total
Great Britain	1951	23,181	865	8,646	9,511	41.1
	1955	23,912	862	9,206	10,068	42.1
Schumann Plan Countries						
W. Germany	1950	21,379	669	7,193	7,862	36.8
France ... ... • ...	1946	20,520	376	4,518	4,894	23.8
Italy	1947	20,080	(13)	5,977	5,990	29.8
Belgium & Luxembourg	1947	3,616	195	1,351	1,546	42.7
Netherlands	1947	3,866	52	925	977	25.2
Total		69,461	1,305	19,964	21,269	30.7
Scandinavia						
Denmark	1950	2,063	4	539	543	26.3
Finland	1950	1,984	6	411	417	21.0
Norway	1950	1,388	9	358	367	26.4
Sweden	1950	3,105	16	972	988	31.8
Total		8,540	35	2,280	2,315	27.3
Other Western European Countries						
Austria	1951	3,361	51	897	948	28.2
Eire	1951	1,272	10	193	203	16.0
Portugal	1950	3,288	26	620	646	19.7
Switzerland	1950	2,156	6	823	829	38.4
Total		10,077	93	2,533	2,626	26.1
Total of W. Europe includ- ing U.K. (1951) ...		111,259	2,298	33,423	35,721	32.1
British (1951) Share of Total W. Europe %		20.8%	37.7%	25.8%	26.6%	
Compare U.S.A. including Alaska	1950	60,104	970	16,118	17,088	28.3

Sources. All except Italy; *United Nations Demographic Yearbook for 1955*, Table 16. Great Britain includes Northern Ireland. Western Germany includes W. Berlin and the Saar. The last column shows producers in Mining and Quarrying and Manufacturing as a percentage of total economically active population. For Italy the figure used for Manufacturing is that given for ' Industry ' in the *Oxford Economic Atlas*, Index, p. 84. For mining the figures for hard-coal and iron ore arise from the *4th General Report of the E.C S.C.* (the true figures must be higher than this).

It is not possible to treat every industry individually, but the figures for the production of coal, steel, and electric power in the various European countries tell the same story about the size of the Common Market. In 1954 the six ' Schumann Plan ' countries produced 242 mn. metric tons of coal, and Britain produced 228 mn. tons, making a total of 470 mn. tons, or 32 per cent of total world production. For comparison, the United States produced 380 mn. tons (25½ per cent of world production) and the Soviet Union 259 mn. tons (17½ per cent of the world total).

TABLE II

Population and Gross National Product of European Countries

Note. 1954 Population in '000s. Gross National Product in 1954, at current prices and in £ Sterling converting at official Exchange rates.

Country or Group	Population (000)	G.N.P. (£mn)	G.N.P. (£ per head)
U.K.	51,200	17,900	350
Schumann Plan Countries			
Western Germany	50,690	12,400	245
France...	43,000	15,700	365
Italy	47,665	7,040	148
Belgium and Luxembourg	9,125	3,200	351
Netherlands	10,615	2,500	236
Total	161,095	40,840	253
Scandinavia			
Denmark	4,406	1,420	322
Finland	4,190	1,290	308
Norway	3,392	1,140	336
Sweden	7,214	2,900	402
Total	19,202	6,750	351
Rest of W. Europe			
Austria	6,969	1,200	172
Eire	2,993	513	171
Greece	7,901	660	84
Portugal	8,693	615	71
Switzerland	4,923	N.A.	N.A.
Iceland	154	63	409
Total	31,633	3,051*	114*
Total of W. Europe including U.K.	263,130	68,541*	266*

Population of other major areas in 1954

U.S.A. (including Alaska)	162,617
U.S.S.R.	214,500 ⎱ Total 307,871
Eastern Europe (excluding U.S.S.R. and Yugoslavia)...	93,371 ⎰

* Excluding Switzerland.

Sources: Population, *U.N. Demographic Yearbook for 1955*, Section 1. Western Germany includes W. Berlin and the Saar. G.N.P., E.C.E. *Economic Survey of Europe in 1955*, pp. 57 *et seq.* (Belgian figures adjusted to allow for Luxembourg), except Eire and Iceland, which are taken from *7th Report of the O.E.E.C.*, Feb. 1956.

In steel the situation is similar: in 1955 the Schumann Plan countries produced 44 mn. tons of crude steel, and Britain produced 19 mn. tons, making a total of 63 mn. tons, or 28 per cent of the world's total steel production. This compares with 80 mn. tons in the United States (36 per cent of the world total), and 41 mn. tons in the U.S.S.R. (18½ per cent of the total).

In 1953 Britain generated 66 billion kilowatt-hours of electric power; the Schumann Plan countries generated 153 billion, and the rest of Western Europe 76 billion, making a total of 295 billion for Western Europe as a whole. This can be compared with 133 billion in the U.S.S.R. and 699 billion kilowatt-hours in the U.S.A. plus Canada (in 1955).

TABLE III

Western Europe's Share in World Production of Coal and Steel
Mn. metric tons, and per cent of total world output

Country	Coal (1954)		Steel (1955)	
	mn. tons	%	mn. tons	%
World Total	1,480	100.0	223	100.0
Schumann Plan Countries (=Coal and Steel Community)	241.7	16.3	43.8	19.7
Great Britain	227.9	15.4	18.8	8.4
S.P. plus Great Britain	469.6	31.7	62.6	28.1
U.S.A.	380.2	25.7	80.1	36.0
U.S.S.R.	259.0	17.5	41.0	18.4

Source: 4th General Report of the Activities of the Community, European Coal and Steel Community, 1956. pp. 79 (Coal) and 52 (Steel). The latest complete year's figures are used. The totals for all Western Europe would be slightly larger than those shown for the E.C.S.C. plus Great Britain, as the output of Sweden, Austria, etc., is not shown here.

TABLE IV

Production of Electric Power in 1953
'000 mn kilowatt-hours and per cent of Western European Total

		%			%
Great Britain	66.0	22.4			
Schumann Plan Countries ...			**Other Western European Countries**		
W. Germany and Saar ...	59.5		Austria 8.8		
France	41.3		Eire 1.3		
Itsly	32.6		Greece 0.9		
Belgium and Luxg. ...	10.7		Portugal 1.4		
Netherlands	9.1		Switzerland 13.5		
Total	153.2	52.0	Total 25.9		8.8
Scandinavia			**Total Western Europe** ... 294.9		100
Denmark	2.4				
Finland	5.4		Compare total U.S.S.R. ... 133.0		
Norway	19.6				
Sweden	22.4				
Total	49.8	16.9			

Source: E.C.E. *Economic Survey of Europe in 1954,* p. 208.

Thus, taking three of the basic industries essential for a modern economy, membership of the European Free Trade Area would mean that Britain formed part of a market over twice her present size measured in terms of coal, $3\frac{1}{2}$ times in terms of steel production, and $4\frac{1}{2}$ times her present size measured in terms of electric power generated.

In considering the possibilities of benefits from freer trade within Western Europe we should first see how much trade is carried on even with the present limitations, which include not only tariffs but quantitative controls, though these have been greatly reduced since 1950 under the O.E.E.C.'s 'trade liberalisation' programme.

TABLE V

Progress in Trade Liberalisation by Britain and the Schumann Plan Countries up to 31st December, 1955

Note. Figures refer to percentage of imports from O.E.E.C. members freed from quantitative controls, average of types of goods currently under private trading, but weighted by their importance in trade in 1948.

Country	Food and foodstuffs	Raw materials	Manufactured products	Total
Target ...	>75	>75	>75	>90
U.K.	89.8	83.6	78.0	84.8*
W. Germany	81.3	98.0	95.6	91.3
France	63.2*	95.7	64.4*	77.5*
Italy	97.6	100.0	98.9	99.1
Benelux	69.0*	98.6	91.8	91.1

Source: O.E.E.C. *7th Annual Report*, Feb. 1956, p. 67.
* Indicates target not reached.

TABLE VI

Exports of Goods and Services per capita and as per cent of G.N.P. in 1954

Country	Exports of goods and services £mn	Exports of goods and services per capita	Exports of goods and services as percent of G.N.P.
Great Britain	4,200	82	23.5
Schumann Plan Countries			
W. Germany	2,690	53	21.7
France	2,380	55	15.2
Italy	810	17	11.5
Belgium and Lux.	1,036	114	32.4
Netherlands	1,280	120	51.2
Total	8,196	51	20.2
Scandinavia			
Denmark	460	104	32.4
Finland	285	68	22.1
Norway	435	128	38.2
Sweden	622	86	21.4
Total	1,802	94	26.7
Other Countries			
Austria	286	41	23.8
Eire	176	59	34.3
Greece	83	10.5	12.6
Iceland	28.5	185	45.2
Portugal	112	13	18.2
Total	685.5	26	22.5
Total W. Europe, incld. G.B.	14,883.5	58	21.7

Source: E.C.E. *Economic Survey of Europe in 1955*, pp. 57 *et seq.*, except for Eire and Iceland for which O.E.E.C. *7th Annual Report*. Population and G.N.P. as in Table II.

We should also consider the importance of international trade to the various members of the Free Trade Area. Comparing total exports with gross national product for various countries in 1954, we find that exports (including exports of services as well as goods) in Britain formed 23½ per cent of the G.N.P., or slightly more than the average for Western Europe as a whole, which was 21½ per cent. For Western Germany, France and Italy the proportion of exports to G.N.P. was lower than in Britain, whereas for Belgium and Luxembourg and the Netherlands it was higher. Within the Schumann Plan group the proportion ranged from 11½ per cent in Italy to 51 per cent in the Netherlands.

It is also of interest to see how much of the trade of the countries of Western Europe was done with each other. Using an average of the proportions of their exports in 1951, 1953 and 1955 going to Great Britain, to the Schumann Plan Countries, and to the whole of Western Europe, including these and other countries, the results are as follows: of the Schumann Plan Countries, the Netherlands had the highest percentage of exports going to Great Britain (13½ per cent), and Western Germany had the lowest (4½ per cent). The Schumann Plan countries sent between 19½ per cent (France) and 39 per cent (Belgium and Luxembourg) to each other, whereas only 12 per cent of Britain's total exports went to Schumann Plan countries. The proportion of total exports going to all Western European countries, including Britain, varied among Schumann Plan countries from 41½ per cent in France to 66 per cent in the Netherlands, while Britain sold 30 per cent of her total exports to all Western European countries. This compares with 45 per cent of British exports in the same years which went to the Sterling Area (excluding Eire).

TABLE VII

Percentage of British Exports going to Various Regions

Note. Exports include re-exports. Eire and Iceland are included in W. Europe and excluded from Sterling Area .

Region	1951	1953	1955	Average
Sterling Area	44.2	44.9	45.4	44.8
Dollar Area	11.6	14.4	13.3	13.1
W. Europe	28.3	30.8	30.9	30.0
Other Countries	15.9	9.9	10.4	12.1

Source: U.N. Statistical Office, *Commodity Trade Statistics* (Series D. Vol. III no. 4 and Vol. V no. 4), Summary Tables for 1953 and 1955. E.C.E. *Economic Survey of Europe* since the war, 1954 Table LV, pp. 300 *et seq.* for 1951. 1951 proportion shows shares of exports to each region valued at 1948 prices: for Areas see notes to Table VIII.

The sources of imports show similar results. Here, on an average of 1953 and 1955, Britain obtained 27 per cent of her imports from Western Europe as a whole, and 11½ per cent from the Schumann Plan Countries; this compares with 39½ per cent from the Sterling Area and 20 per cent from the Dollar Area. The Schumann Plan Countries obtained 6 per cent of their total imports from Britain, and 47½ per cent from Western Europe (including both Great Britain and each other); again the proportions taken from Britain ranged from 4 per cent (Germany) to 9 per cent (the Netherlands), and the proportion from Western Europe as a whole from 31 per cent (France) to 58 per cent (Belgium and Luxembourg).

In considering the possible effects on British industry of entry into a Free Trade Area, we also need to examine the composition of trade between Britain and Europe. In 1951[1] the Schumann Plan Countries took 10 per cent of Britain's total exports, and the whole of Western Europe, including these, took 28 per cent of the total. A tenth of Britain's exports, both to the Schumann Plan countries and to the whole of Western Europe consisted of raw materials, which were very largely the produce of Commonwealth countries shipped to Britain and re-exported. The same can be said of much of the 6½ per cent of her exports to the Schumann Plan Countries which consisted of food, drink and tobacco.

Exports of goods which were actually produced in Britain (though almost all of her exports have some imported materials in them, directly or indirectly) can be classified as follows, the percentages referring to proportions of manufactured exports, *i.e.* total exports *minus* raw materials, food, drink and tobacco, and ' unspecified '. The largest group was machinery, forming 22 per cent of her home-produced exports to all areas—as of British exports to Western Europe as a whole and to the Sterling Area. The Schumann Plan countries, however, took a relatively large proportion (26 per cent) of British exports to them in machinery.[2]

The next largest group was textiles, with 21 per cent of the total to all areas; the whole of Western Europe took slightly less from this group (20 per cent), and within Western Europe the Schumann Plan Countries took only 14 per cent in textiles; 22 per cent of British exports to the Sterling Area, on the other hand, consisted of textiles.

The third major group of exports was transport equipment and private motor vehicles. These accounted for 21 per cent of total exports, but 24½ per cent of exports to Western Europe as a whole fell within this group, though it accounted for only 22½ per cent of exports to the Schumann Plan countries; while the Sterling Area took 21 per cent from these groups. These figures however cover a major difference between private cars and other forms of transport equipment; private cars accounted for a quarter of this group, in total exports, at 5¼ per cent of total exports, but whereas the Sterling Area took 5½ per cent of British exports to it in cars, and only 15 per cent in other transport equipment, Western Europe took only 3½ per cent in cars, but 21 per cent in other transport equipment.

The other groups of exports were metals and metal manufactures, with 13 per cent of the total, chemicals with 8 per cent and ' other manufactures '

---

[1] 1951 is in many ways a bad year to choose since German recovery from the War was far from complete, but it is the latest year for which the author has been able to obtain figures classified by suitable commodity groups and destinations.

[2] See the notes to Table XI for the limitations on the significance of these figures.

Table VIII

Exports of Great Britain and the Schumann Plan Countries, by Destinations

Section I—Million $ (See Notes)

Exporting Country	Total Exports					To Western Europe				
	1938	1948	1951	1953	1955	1938	1948	1951	1953	1955
Great Britain	5,184	6,377	8,309	7,230	8,135	1,618	1,870	2,350	2,226	2,512
Western Germany	4,409	701	4,032	4,412	6,134	2,681	615	2,608	2,900	3,970
France	2,279	2,071	4,355	4,019	4,797	1,157	811	1,591	1,655	2,212
Italy	1,358	1,068	1,719	1,488	1,857	574	444	941	785	1,054
Belgium and Luxembourg ...	1,856	1,684	2,458	2,259	2,779	1,202	1,039	1,536	1,412	1,840
Netherlands	1,658	1,004	2,466	2,121	2,687	1,136	686	1,675	1,344	1,786
Total Schumann Plan ...	11,561	6,527	15,030	14,299	18,254	6,750	3,595	8,352	8,096	10,862

Section II. Percentage of Exports to all Destinations

Exporting Country	Total Exports					To Western Europe				
	1938	1948	1951	1953	1955	1938	1948	1951	1953	1955
Great Britain	100.0	100.0	100.0	100.0	100.0	31.2	29.3	28.3	30.8	30.9
Western Germany	100.0	100.0	100.0	100.0	100.0	60.8	87.9	64.7	65.8	64.8
France	100.0	100.0	100.0	100.0	100.0	50.7	39.2	36.5	41.2	46.1
Italy	100.0	100.0	100.0	100.0	100.0	42.3	41.6	54.8	52.9	56.7
Belgium and Luxembourg ...	100.0	100.0	100.0	100.0	100.0	64.8	61.7	62.5	62.5	66.3
Netherlands	100.0	100.0	100.0	100.0	100.0	68.5	68.4	67.9	63.4	66.4
Total Schumann Plan ...	100.0	100.0	100.0	100.0	100.0	58.4	55.1	55.6	56.6	59.5

Section I—Million $

Exporting Country	To Schumann Plan					To Great Britain					To Other Western Europe				
	1938	1948	1951	1953	1955	1938	1948	1951	1953	1955	1938	1948	1951	1953	1955
Great Britain	713	624	842	941	1,052	—	—	—	—	—	905	1,246	1,508	1,285	1,460
Western Germany	1,093	369	1,172	1,317	1,767	295	72	236	188	245	1,293	174	1,201	1,395	1,958
France	582	374	674	747	1,170	275	154	370	217	353	300	283	548	691	689
Italy	309	123	369	297	436	75	85	234	108	135	190	235	338	380	483
Belgium and Luxembourg	717	522	849	867	1,240	257	152	244	176	179	228	366	443	369	421
Netherlands	551	320	878	765	1,029	390	144	411	228	332	195	222	386	351	425
Total Schumann Plan	3,252	1,709	3,941	3,993	5,642	1,292	607	1,495	917	1,244	2,206	1,280	2,916	3,186	3,976

Section II. Percentage of Exports to all Destinations

Exporting Country	To Schumann Plan					To Great Britain					To Other Western Europe				
	1938	1948	1951	1953	1955	1938	1948	1951	1953	1955	1938	1948	1951	1953	1955
Great Britain	13.8	9.8	10.1	13.0	12.9	—	—	—	—	—	17.5	19.5	18.1	17.8	18.0
Western Germany	24.8	52.7	29.1	29.8	28.8	6.7	10.2	5.9	4.3	4.0	29.3	24.9	29.8	31.6	31.9
France	25.6	18.0	15.4	18.6	24.4	12.1	7.5	8.5	5.4	7.4	13.2	13.7	12.6	17.2	14.4
Italy	22.8	11.6	21.5	20.0	23.5	5.5	8.0	13.6	7.3	7.3	14.0	22.0	19.7	25.6	26.0
Belgium and Luxembourg	38.6	31.0	34.6	38.4	44.6	13.9	9.0	10.0	7.8	6.4	12.2	21.7	18.0	16.3	15.1
Netherlands	33.3	31.9	35.6	36.0	38.3	23.5	14.3	16.7	10.7	12.4	11.8	22.1	15.7	16.5	15.8
Total Schumann Plan	28.2	26.2	26.2	28.0	30.9	11.2	9.3	10.0	6.4	6.8	19.1	19.6	19.4	22.3	21.8

Sources. 1938, 1948 and 1951 from E.C.E. *Economic Survey of Europe since the War,* 1954, Table LV, p. 300 *et seq.* These figures are in 1948 dollars; the figures for 1938 and 1951 will thus understate the true share of exports to any area if the average price of these was higher in 1938 or 1951 than the average price of all exports, relative to 1948; but as the composition of exports to various destinations was broadly similar (see tables X to XII below) this source of error should not be serious.

For 1953 and 1955 the figures are taken from United Nations *Commodity Trade Statistics,* Jan.–Dec. of these years, summary tables. (*U.N. Statistical Papers,* Series D, Vol. III No. 4 (1953) and Vol. V No. 4 (1955). These figures are in current dollars: thus the table above cannot be used to measure the growth of trade to various destinations. The Schumann Plan Countries' total exports include exports to each other. Total exports to Western Europe include exports to Great Britain, to the Schumann Plan Countries, and to ' other Western European Countries' which comprises Austria, Denmark, Eire, Finland, Greece, Iceland, Norway, Portugal, Spain, Sweden, Switzerland, Turkey and Yugoslavia.

TABLE IX

Sources of Imports, 1953 and 1955

Importing Country	Total World	Dollar Area	Sterling Area (exclg. Britain & Eire)	West'n Europe (inclg. Britain & Eire)	S.P. Countries	Britain	O.W.E.	Other
1953	$ mn	$ mn	$ mn	$ mn	$ mn	$ mn	$ mn	$ mn
Great Britain	9,366	1,765	3,889	2,481	975	—	1,506	1,231
Western Germany	3,809	645	451	1,993	956	154	883	720
France	4,166	486	913	1,230	667	191	372	1,537
Italy ...	2,395	389	464	1,112	529	185	398	430
Belgium & Luxembourg	2,423	372	237	1,393	934	219	240	421
Netherlands	2,354	324	215	1,343	882	221	240	472
Total Schumann Plan	15,147	2,216	2,280	7,071	3,968	970	2,133	3,580
1955								
Great Britain	10,881	2,348	4,105	3,031	1,351	—	1,680	1,397
Western Germany ...	5,793	1,173	663	2,927	1,502	206	1,219	1,030
France	4,688	571	898	1,533	930	179	424	1,686
Italy	2,705	467	518	1,232	646	144	442	488
Belgium & Luxembourg	2,844	429	263	1,677	1,168	241	268	475
Netherlands	3,208	594	245	1,886	1,305	273	308	483
Total Schumann Plan ...	19,238	3,234	2,587	9,255	5,551	1,043	2,661	4,162
1953	%	%	%	%	%	%	%	%
Great Britain	100	18.8	41.5	26.5	10.4	—	16.1	13.1
Western Germany ...	100	16.9	11.8	52.3	25.1	4.0	23.2	18.9
France	100	11.7	21.9	29.5	16.0	4.6	8.9	36.9
Italy	100	16.2	19.4	46.5	22.1	7.7	16.6	18.0
Belgium & Luxembourg	100	15.3	9.8	57.5	38.5	9.0	9.9	17.4
Netherlands	100	13.8	9.1	57.0	37.4	9.4	10.2	20.0
Total Schumann Plan	100	14.6	15.0	46.6	26.2	6.4	14.1	23.6
1955								
Great Britain	100	21.6	37.8	27.9	12.4	—	15.5	12.8
Western Germany ...	100	20.2	11.4	50.5	25.9	3.6	21.0	17.8
France	100	12.2	19.2	32.7	19.8	3.8	9.0	36.0
Italy	100	17.3	19.1	45.6	23.9	5.3	16.3	18.0
Belgium & Luxembourg	100	15.1	9.2	58.8	41.0	8.5	9.4	16.7
Netherlands	100	18.5	7.6	58.8	40.7	8.5	9.6	15.1
Total Schumann Plan ...	100	16.8	13.4	48.1	28.8	5.4	13.8	21.6

S.P. Countries = Schumann Plan Countries.
O.W.E. = Other Western Europe.
Notes. Imports from Great Britain, Eire and Iceland are included under Western Europe and excluded from Sterling Area figures. Other Western Europe = Austria, Denmark, Eire, Finland, Iceland, Norway, Portugal, Spain, Sweden, Switzerland, Turkey and Yugoslavia.
Source: U.N. Statistical Papers. Series D, Vol. III, No. 4 (1953) and Vol. V, No. 4 (1955), *Commodity Trade Statistics*, Summary Tables.

TABLE X

Commodity Composition of British Exports, 1938, 1948 and 1951.
1948 U.S. $mn.

Commodity Group	Destination, 1938					Destination, 1948					Destination 1951				
	S.P.	O.W.E.	T.W.E.	S.A.	W.T.	S.P.	O.W.E.	T.W.E.	S.A.	W.T.	S.P.	O.W.E.	T.W.E.	S.A.	W.T.
1. Food, Drink & Tobacco	21.4	35.0	56.4	103.2	369.7	38.4	54.4	92.8	108.9	395.8	54.5	40.8	95.3	168.6	506.7
2. Raw Materials	277.0	254.1	531.1	27.8	927.0	70.9	110.9	181.8	27.2	361.4	90.4	132.2	222.6	63.1	499.4
3. Metals & Metal Manufactures	33.7	69.5	103.2	262.5	546.0	76.3	164.3	240.6	317.9	817.8	77.8	150.3	228.1	418.7	929.3
4. Machinery	59.3	68.5	127.8	335.0	653.5	124.1	226.5	350.6	590.5	1,314.6	169.2	249.5	418.7	753.4	1,569.0
5. Personal Cars	1.7	8.0	9.7	28.8	51.8	24.5	27.6	52.1	102.6	224.5	25.8	42.6	68.4	190.4	358.9
6. Other Transport Equipment	20.7	49.3	70.0	144.7	290.3	81.4	179.8	261.2	283.7	714.6	120.9	273.5	394.4	501.6	1,122.9
7. Chemicals	18.0	33.7	51.7	100.8	216.2	33.0	63.0	96.0	135.6	337.0	51.0	85.9	136.9	240.7	572.3
8. Textiles	97.6	212.3	309.8	525.3	1,476.5	44.5	173.3	217.8	612.5	1,308.3	90.7	286.0	376.7	757.8	1,513.0
9. Other Manufactures	54.5	75.4	129.9	221.0	533.0	55.0	140.7	195.7	307.9	743.4	108.8	161.9	270.7	482.3	1,093.0
10. Unspecified	129.0	99.1	228.1	99.4	119.6	76.0	105.5	181.5	94.2	159.5	53.7	84.5	138.2	102.0	145.0
Total	712.9	904.9	1,617.7	1,848.5	5,183.6	624.1	1,246.0	1,870.1	2,581.0	6,376.9	842.8	1,507.2	2,350.0	3,678.6	8,309.5
Total of 3–9	285.5	516.7	802.1	1,618.1	3,767.3	438.8	975.2	1,414.0	2,350.7	5,460.2	644.2	1,249.7	1,893.9	3,344.9	7,158.4
Total of 1, 2, 10	427.4	388.2	815.6	230.4	1,416.3	185.3	270.8	456.1	230.2	916.7	198.6	257.5	456.1	333.7	1,151.1

S.P. = Schumann Plan Countries; O.W.E. = Other Western Europe; T.W.E. = Total Western Europe; S.A. = Sterling Area; W.T. = World Total.

Source. E.C.E. *Economic Survey of Europe Since the War*, Table LV, pp. 300 *et seq.* 'Schumann Plan Countries' figure includes exports to E. Germany—'Other Western Europe' comprises Austria, Denmark, Eire, Finland, Greece, Iceland, Norway, Portugal, Spain, Sweden, Switzerland, Turkey and Yugoslavia. Sterling Area excludes Eire and Iceland.

with 15 per cent; there were no important differences between the Sterling Area, Western Europe, and the Schumann Plan Countries in the proportions they took in these groups.

It is also possible to analyse in the same way the composition of exports in 1951 from the Schumann Plan Countries to Britain: 37 per cent of these consisted of food, drink, and tobacco, and a further $13\frac{1}{2}$ per cent of raw materials: thus only a half of the Schumann Plan Countries' exports to Britain consisted of manufactures, and though some of these countries' non-industrial exports to Britain consisted of local agricultural produce, and only part of re-exports from their dependencies or other tropical countries, both these groups, and ' unspecified ', are excluded in taking the percentages given below.

The largest portion of the Schumann Plan group's remaining exports to Britain was textiles (35 per cent).[1] These, and two other major groups, chemicals with $15\frac{1}{2}$ per cent and ' other manufactures ' with 18 per cent formed larger parts of exports to Britain than of exports by the Schumann Plan Countries to the world as a whole (including each other). Metals and manufactures with 20 per cent, and machinery, with 10 per cent, though forming a substantial share of exports to Britain, were less important than in these countries' exports to the world as a whole, while both private motor vehicles and other transport equipment were unimportant in both senses (this was in 1951 before the Volkswagen sales campaign became really strong).

One species of relevant information concerning the consequences of an abolition of tariffs is their height. This information is not readily available, since tariff schedules are of extreme complexity; thus taking an average of the *ad valorem* duties payable on the different tariff headings in each commodity group involves 'weighting' the varieties of the commodities concerned in proportion to the ingenuity with which they have been sub-classified; while weighting in accordance with trade values is difficult because published trade figures do not correspond to the divisions of tariff schedules. Even if the latter method could be pursued the results would be of dubious significance because the weighting of any tariff on a given heading is diminished by its very effectiveness in restricting trade—indeed where trade in an article is effectively prevented by a tariff, its weighting in such an index is zero. Obtaining comparable estimates of the tariffs of various European countries on even one section of a tariff (out of about 16 sections of manufactured goods) would thus form a considerable research project.

However, in order that readers may form some estimation of the order of magnitude of European tariffs, Table XVI reproduces the results of a Study published in 1952 by the Council of Europe, showing the proportion of tariff *headings* (not trade) on which the *ad valorem* duty payable was over 10 per cent, in various commodity groups for the major European countries

---

[1] Percentages in this paragraph refer to shares in manufactured exports.

TABLE XI

Commodity Composition of British Exports, 1938, 1948 and 1951

Section I

Percentage of total exports of Groups 3 to 9 in each commodity group

Commodity Group	Destination, 1938					Destination, 1948					Destination, 1951				
	S.P.	O.W.E.	T.W.E.	S.A.	W.T.	S.P.	O.W.E.	T.W.E.	S.A.	W.T.	S.P.	O.W.E.	T.W.E.	S.A.	W.T.
3. Metals and Metal Manufactures	11.8	13.5	12.9	16.3	14.5	17.4	16.9	17.0	13.5	15.0	12.1	12.0	12.0	12.5	12.9
4. Machinery	20.8	13.3	15.9	20.7	17.3	28.3	23.2	24.8	25.2	24.0	26.3	19.9	22.1	22.5	21.9
5. Personal Cars	.6	1.5	1.2	1.8	1.4	5.6	2.8	3.7	4.4	4.1	4.0	3.5	3.6	5.7	5.0
6. Other Transport Equipment	7.3	9.5	8.7	9.0	7.7	18.5	18.4	18.5	12.1	13.0	18.7	21.9	20.8	15.0	15.7
7. Chemicals	6.3	6.5	6.5	6.2	5.7	7.5	6.5	6.8	5.8	6.2	7.9	6.9	7.2	7.2	8.0
8. Textiles	34.3	41.1	38.6	32.6	39.2	10.1	17.8	15.4	26.1	23.9	14.0	22.9	19.9	22.6	21.1
9. Other Manufactures	19.1	14.6	16.2	13.7	14.1	12.5	14.4	13.8	13.1	13.6	16.8	12.9	14.3	14.4	15.3
Total of Groups 3–9	100.0	100.0	100.0	100.0	100.0	100.0	100.0	100.0	100.0	100.0	100.0	100.0	100.0	100.0	100.0
Section II															
Share of Groups 3–9 in total of all Groups	40.0	57.0	49.5	87.5	72.7	70.2	78.3	75.6	91.1	85.6	76.4	82.9	80.5	90.9	86.1
Shares in total exports of all Groups of:															
1. Food, Drink & Tobacco	3.0	3.9	3.5	5.6	7.1	6.2	4.4	5.0	4.2	6.2	6.5	2.7	4.1	4.6	6.1
2. Raw Materials	38.8	28.2	32.9	1.5	17.9	11.4	8.9	9.7	1.1	5.7	10.7	8.8	9.5	1.7	6.0
10. Unspecified	18.1	11.0	14.1	5.4	2.3	12.2	8.5	9.7	3.6	2.5	6.4	5.6	5.9	2.8	1.7

S.P. = Schumann Plan Countries; O.W.E. = Other Western Europe; T.W.E. = Total Western Europe; S.A. = Sterling Area; W.T. = World Total.

Section I. Groups 1, 'Food, Drink and Tobacco', and 2, 'Raw Materials' are excluded in order to reduce the influence of re-exports, and Group 10, 'Unspecified', since it has obviously been used to contain residual errors.

Section II. Figures give, e.g., U.K. exports of goods in Group 1 to the Schumann Plan Countries as a per cent of total U.K. exports to Schumann Plan Countries, in each year.

Both Sections. Source as for Table X. As the figures in Table X show values at 1948 prices, in 1938 and 1951 the above table understates the relative importance, at current prices of exports of goods whose prices relative to the average of all export prices were higher in these years than in 1948.

TABLE XII

Importance of Commodity Groups in British Exports to various Destinations, relative to their share in British Exports to all Destinations

Commodity Group	1938				1948				1951				Group
	S.P.	O.W.E.	T.W.E.	S.A.	S.P.	O.W.E.	T.W.E.	S.A.	S.P.	O.W.E.	T.W.E.	S.A.	
1. Food, Drink & Tobacco ...	.42	.55	.49	.79	1.00	.71	.81	.68	1.07	.44	.67	.75	1
2. Raw Materials	2.17	1.57	1.84	.08	2.00	1.58	1.70	.19	1.78	1.48	1.58	.28	2
3. Metals and Metal Manufactures	.81	.93	.89	1.12	1.16	1.13	1.13	.90	.94	.93	.93	.97	3
4. Machinery	1.20	.77	.92	1.20	1.18	.97	1.03	1.05	1.20	.91	1.01	1.03	4
5. Personal Cars	.43	1.07	.86	1.28	1.36	.68	.90	1.07	.80	.70	.72	1.14	5
6. Other Transport Equipment	.95	1.23	1.13	1.17	1.42	1.41	1.42	.93	1.19	1.39	1.32	.95	6
7. Chemicals	1.10	1.14	1.14	1.09	1.21	1.05	1.10	.94	.99	.86	.90	.90	7
8. Textiles	.88	1.05	.99	.83	.42	.75	.65	1.09	.66	1.08	.94	1.07	8
9. Other Manufactures ...	1.35	1.03	1.15	.97	.92	1.06	1.02	.96	1.10	.84	.93	.94	9
10. Unspecified	Figures not significant because of errors				—	—	—	—	—	—	—	—	10

S.P. = Schumann Plan; O.W.E. = Other Western Europe.; T.W.E. = Total Western Europe; S.A. = Sterling Area.

Sources as in Tables X and XI. The figures are ratios. The numerator is the share of exports to a particular area (*e.g.* Schumann Plan countries) taken by a particular commodity group (*e.g.* personal cars): the denominator is the share of total exports to all areas taken by the commodity group in question. To illustrate, personal cars in 1951 were 4 per cent of the total exports (groups 3—9) to S.P. countries; personal cars were 5 per cent of total exports of the same group to all destinations: the ratio is therefore 4—5, *i.e.* .80 For groups 1 and 2, the proportions used are those of Table XI, Section II: for groups 3—9, the proportions used are those shown in Table XI, Section I.

TABLE XIII

Total Exports of the Schumann Plan Countries

Commodity Group	1948 $mn.			Percentages of Total			Percentages of Total of Groups 3–9			Group
	1938	1948	1951	1938	1948	1951	1938	1948	1951	
1. Food, Drink and Tobacco	1,427.8	921.5	2,400.0	12.4	14.1	16.0	—	—	—	1
2. Raw Materials	2,377.4	1,163.3	1,941.3	20.6	17.9	12.9	—	—	—	2
3. Metals and Metal Manufactures	1,860.9	1,199.6	3,260.3	16.1	18.4	21.7	24.4	27.3	30.9	3
4. Machinery	1,113.3	589.8	1,629.9	9.6	9.0	10.8	14.6	13.4	15.5	4
5. Private Motor Cars	113.2	102.2	275.7	1.0	1.6	1.8	1.5	2.3	2.6	5
6. Other Transport Equipment	446.1	244.0	634.7	3.9	3.7	4.2	5.9	5.6	6.0	6
7. Chemicals	1,017.0	445.7	1,284.0	8.8	6.8	8.5	13.4	10.2	12.2	7
8. Textiles	1,748.8	1,193.7	2,145.3	15.1	18.3	14.3	23.0	27.2	20.4	8
9. Other Manufactures	1,319.0	610.0	1,312.7	11.4	9.4	8.7	17.3	13.9	12.5	9
10. Unspecified	137.7	48.6	145.9	1.2	0.7	1.0	—	—	—	10
Total	11,561.2	6,518.4	15,027.8	100.0	100.0	100.0	—	—	—	Total
3–9	7,618.3	4,385.0	10,540.6	65.9	67.3	70.2	100.0	100.0	100.0	3–9
1, 2, 10	3,942.9	2,133.4	4,487.2	34.1	32.7	29.8	—	—	—	1, 2, 10

Source. As for Tables X and XI. The same limitations apply to the figures for the commodity composition of trade in 1938 and in 1951 since these are given at 1948 prices.

TABLE XIV

Schumann Plan Countries' Exports to Great Britain

Commodity Group	1938 $ mn			Percentages of Total			Percentages of total of Groups 3–9			Group
	1938	1948	1951	1938	1948	1951	1938	1948	1951	
1. Food, Drink and Tobacco ...	287.9	197.7	556.7	22.4	32.6	37.2	—	—	—	1
2. Raw Materials ...	271.0	110.3	204.0	21.1	18.2	13.6	—	—	—	2
3. Metals and Metal Manufactures	163.9	67.0	145.0	12.7	11.0	9.7	23.0	24.0	20.2	3
4. Machinery	70.3	11.4	71.7	5.5	1.9	4.8	9.8	4.1	10.0	4
5. Private Motor cars ...	4.5	2.1	3.1	0.4	0.3	0.2	0.6	0.8	0.4	5
6. Other Transport Equipment	12.4	2.2	5.9	1.0	0.4	0.4	1.7	0.8	0.8	6
7. Chemicals	75.7	27.5	110.1	5.9	4.5	7.4	10.6	9.9	15.4	7
8. Textiles	181.5	113.3	252.7	14.1	18.7	16.9	25.4	40.7	35.2	8
9. Other Manufactures ...	206.7	55.1	130.1	16.1	9.1	8.7	29.0	19.8	18.1	9
10. Unspecified	12.7	20.0	15.4	1.0	3.3	1.0	—	—	—	10
Total	1,286.6	606.6	1,494.7	100.0	100.0	100.0	—	—	—	Total
3–9	715.0	278.6	718.6	55.5	46.0	48.0	100	100	100	3–9
1, 2, 10	571.6	328.0	776.1	44.5	54.0	52.0	—	—	—	1, 2, 10

Source: As for Tables X and XI.

TABLE XV

Importance of Commodity Groups in Schumann Plan Countries' Exports to Great Britain, relative to their share in Schumann Plan Countries' Exports to all Destinations

Commodity Group	1938	1948	1951
1. Food, Drink and Tobacco	1.81	2.31	2.32
2. Raw Materials	1.02	1.02	1.05
3. Metals and Metal Manufactures	.94	.88	.65
4. Machinery	.68	.31	.65
5. Private Motor Cars	.40	.35	.15
6. Other Transport Equipment	.29	.14	.13
7. Chemicals	.79	.97	1.26
8. Textiles	1.11	1.49	1.72
9. Other Manufactures...	1.68	1.42	1.46
10. Unspecified	Figures not Significant.		

Notes. Source as for Tables X and XI. The figures in this table are calculated similarly to those in Table XII. They are ratios showing percentage of Schumann Plan Countries' exports to Great Britain in a particular commodity group divided by percentage of Schumann Plan Countries' exports to all destinations in that group. For groups 1 and 2 the figures are based on shares of these groups in total exports; for groups 3–9 they are based on shares in the total of these groups, *i.e.* of exports of manufactures.

(the most important change since then has been the introduction of temporary reductions of about a third on most items of the German tariff). The results of this study suggest that tariff levels tended to vary not only between countries, and between commodity groups, but also in the relative intensity of protection of different groups in the various countries.

Thus we see that even under the restrictions in force in 1951, an important part of the trade of both Britain and the other Western European countries consisted of selling manufactured goods to each other, and there would be more scope for this if trade within Western Europe were not subject to tariffs; but as the Sterling Area accounted for more British exports than Western Europe in every group but raw materials (which were largely re-exports), it is equally clear that Britain should consider very carefully the effects on trade with the Commonwealth of joining any 'European' Common Market: the Government's proposals that Britain should move towards free trade with Western Europe in non-agricultural products, but without being obliged to adopt the Customs Union tariffs with other countries, are designed to safeguard trade with the Commonwealth.

There are however several possible grounds for opposing British entry even into a Free Trade Area in Western Europe. Whether these are strong enough to justify staying out of any European agreement on Free Trade, or whether the difficulties they raise could be overcome can only be determined by a much wider study of them than is possible here.

All that can be attempted here is to indicate in qualitative terms what the objections to the Free Trade Area are. They fall under three heads—the dangers of dislocation and unemployment in particular industries, the risk of reductions in the standard of living of workers in the richer countries if freer trade or movement of labour is encouraged,

TABLE XVI

Proportions of Tariff Headings with Duty of 11 per cent or over in Various Commodity Groups

Description of Groups	No.	Great Britain	Average S.P.	W.G.	Fr.	It.	Blux.	Average Scan.	Den.	Nor.	Swe.	Austria	No.
Minerals, Earths, Coal, Stone and Petroleum ...	1	17*	16	25*	16	20	2	3	0	7	3	27*	1
Non-Ferrous Metals ...	2	68	51	40	70	97*	17	5	1	12	2	64*	2
Chemical Products ...	3	69	59*	43*	90	91*	12	30	14*	36	40	24*	3
Raw Textiles ...	4	54	61*	62*	64	74	44	14	13	12	17	59*	4
Hides and Leather, Leather Produce, Fur Skins and Furs ...	5	64	61	56	73	86	30	27	41	31	8	29	5
Timber and Wood Products ...	6	50	63*	79*	60	90	22	19	8	40	10	83*	6
Iron, Cast Iron and Steel ...	7	94	68	72	85	97	19	8	2	16	6	90*	7
Electrical Apparatus and Machinery	8	100	69*	62	90	100*	22	34	6	77	26	83*	8
Cement, Ceramics and Glassware ...	9	61	72*	56*	89	93*	50	29	20	47	20	90*	9
Transport Material ...	10	87	75*	59	89	97*	60	41	0	83	39	97*	10
Plastics, Rubber and their Products	11	47	76*	84*	97*	92*	36	39	3	74	41	87*	11
Tools, Cutlery and Products of Base Metals ...	12	99	77	54	99	99*	56	22	11	47	7	88*	12
Optical, Photographic and Precision Instruments ...	13	100	80*	63	100	100*	55	24	7	58	8	75	13
Paper and Cardboard ...	14	89	89*	97*	93	93	78	8	6	13	5	78*	14
Finished Textiles ...	15	93*	95*	95*	99*	98*	90	42	38	47	41	90*	15
Carriages, Motor Cars, Tractors, Cycles and Land Vehicles...	16	100	97*	98*	98*	92*	100	51	7	76	71	96*	16
Average ...	—	71	68*	65*	82	87*	43	25	11	42	21	72*	—

Averages for Schumann Plan Countries are unweighted averages of W. Germany, France, Italy and Benelux. Average for Scandinavia is an unweighted average of Denmark, Norway and Sweden. National Averages are unweighted average of 16 commodity groups (which do not correspond to the groups used in the trade tables). The groups are arranged in ascending order of the average of Schumann Plan countries. Percentages refer to headings and *not* to trade; groups over their national average in italics; * indicates that 5 per cent or more items in the group had tariff rates of 36 per cent or over. Source, *A Low Tariff Club*, Council of Europe, 1952.

and the risk that the adoption of free trade would mean that in deciding on monetary and fiscal policies (*i.e.* investment and government expenditure) safeguarding the balance of payments might have to take priority over maintaining full employment, and general 'deflation' might be the only means left of cutting imports. If deflation proceeded *via* a cut in investment, or induced a decrease in investment through its effects on demand, it would also hinder the future growth of the national income. Britain is not, of course, the only country concerned which needs to worry about these things, nor would freer trade do more than accentuate problems which have to be faced in a changing world anyway, but it is as well to know what the dangers are.

As regards the possibility that some British industries might be injured by competition from Europe, we can only consider a few examples. In the motor-car industry, for example, there are very great advantages in larger-scale production; this is clearly shown by the extreme cheapness of comparable American cars relative to British, and equally by the success of the Volkswagen, which has made up by the duration of its run of output of one basic model for the small size, relative to the United States motor industry, of the market available to it.

TABLE XVII

Production and Trade in Passenger Cars in 1955, in '000s

Major Producing Countries	Pro-duction	Regis-tration of new cars	Exports	Imports	Net exports	Net exports as % of pro-duction
Great Britain	887.6	500.9	373.3	11.6	361.7	40.8
G.B. as per cent of total of W. Germany, France and Italy	59.6	51.2			69.3	
Western Germany	705.5	377.2	357.3	16.8	340.5	48.3
France	552.1	440.2	132.8	10.0	122.8	22.2
Italy	230.9	161.6	61.2	3.0	58.2	25.2
Total of W.G., F. and I. ...	1488.5	979.0	551.3	29.8	521.5	35.0
Other Countries			Overseas Exports of all countries shown ... = 424.6			
Sweden		127.7	Imports from U.S.A. 52.6			
Belgium		74.9	Net Overseas Exports 372.0			
Switzerland		51.2				
Austria		42.3				
Denmark[1]		28.5				
Eire		23.7				
Finland		15.2				
Norway[1]		14.9				
Total		378.4				

Source : E.C.E. *Bulletin for Europe.* Aug. 1956, p. 9. Discrepancies between total 'production 'and ' consumption' figures shown arise from changes in stocks, and incomplete coverage of countries (esp. omission of Netherlands figures).
[1] Figures refer to Net Imports.

TABLE XVIII
Shares of Western Europe's Car Market in 1955

Country	Consumed by:		Supplied by:	
	'000s	%	'000s	%
Great Britain	500.9	22.0	887.6	36.6
Western Germany, France and Italy	979.0	42.8	1,488.5	61.3
Rest of Western Europe ...	378.4	16.5		
Overseas	424.6	18.6		
U.S.A.			52.6	2.2
Total	2,282.9	100.0	2,428.7	100.0

Source. As for Table XVII.

In 1955 total production of private cars was 890,000 in Britain, and 1,490,000 in Germany, France and Italy combined. All these countries exported far more than they imported, with an export surplus of 360,000 cars from Britain and 520,000 from Germany, France and Italy. Of these ' net exports ' over 380,000 went to other Western European Countries, and over 370,000 to overseas countries. Thus freer trade in cars might mean a danger of European producers capturing part of the British home market: this would worsen the present problems of the motor industry (though full free trade would not start at once, and under the present proposals there would be 12 or 15 years to adjust). On the other hand, staying out of the Free Trade Area would not protect British exporters against European

TABLE XIX
Exports, Imports and Net Exports of Textiles in 1954
In million U.S. $ Net Imports —ve

Country	Exports	Imports	Net Exports	Net Exports as % of Exports
Great Britain	1,012	217	795	78.5
Schumann Plan Countries				
W. Germany	334	244	90	27.0
France	557	52	505	90.7
Italy	313	50	263	84.0
Belgium and Luxg.	327	120	207	63.3
Netherlands	223	187	36	16.2
Total	1,754	653	1,101	62.7
Other Countries				
Switzerland	174	91	83	47.7
Austria	66	37	29	44.0
Denmark	16	117	—101	—
Norway	11	98	—87	—
Sweden	24	170	—146	—
Greece	2	28	—26	—
Total	293	541	—248	—
Total Western Europe ...	3,059	1,411	1,648	53.9

Source. E.C.E. *Economic Survey of Europe in 1955*, p. 25.

TABLE XX

Per Capita Consumption and Investment in Great Britain, Western Germany, France and Italy, 1950—1955
(in $ at 1950 European Prices)

Country	Year	Cons.	Investment Total	Investment P.D.	Total	Inv. as % of Total	P.D. as % of Inv.	Cons. as % of G.B.	Inv. as % of G.B.	P.D. as % of G.B.
Great Britain	1950	699	133	86	832	16.0	64.5	—	—	—
	1951	687	131	85	818	16.0	65.0	—	—	—
	1952	678	129	78	807	16.0	60.5	—	—	—
	1953	701	146	86	847	17.2	59.0	—	—	—
	1954	729	153	90	882	17.3	58.8	—	—	—
	1955	757	168	—	925	18.2	—	—	—	—
Western Germany	1950	423	117	62	540	21.7	53.0	60.5	88.0	72.1
	1951	449	126	67	575	21.9	53.2	65.5	96.3	78.8
	1952	479	129	69	608	21.2	53.5	70.7	100.0	88.5
	1953	518	147	75	665	22.1	51.0	73.9	100.7	87.2
	1954	551	164	85	715	22.9	51.8	75.6	107.3	94.5
	1955	591	189	102	780	24.2	54.0	78.1	112.5	—
France	1950	529	125	72	654	19.1	57.6	75.8	94.0	83.7
	1951	550	131	76	681	19.2	58.0	80.2	100.0	89.3
	1952	562	123	73	685	18.0	59.4	82.8	95.3	93.7
	1953	578	123	74	701	17.6	60.2	82.5	84.3	86.0
	1954	604	131	77	735	17.8	58.8	82.9	85.6	85.6
	1955	639	140	83	779	18.0	59.2	84.4	83.3	—
Italy	1950	283	60	—	343	17.5	—	40.5	45.1	—
	1951	288	66	—	354	18.6	—	41.9	50.3	—
	1952	293	73	—	366	19.9	—	43.2	56.6	—
	1953	308	77	—	385	20.0	—	44.0	52.8	—
	1954	316	81	—	397	20.4	—	43.3	52.9	—
	1955	330	92	—	422	21.8	—	43.6	54.8	—

Cons. = Consumption; P.D. = Producers' Durables; Inv. = Investment; G.B. = Great Britain.
Notes. Investment = Gross Investment. 'Totals' cannot be treated as per capita national income as they do not allow for government expenditure or balance of payments.
Source. E.C.E. Economic Survey of Europe in 1955, p. 43.

competition either in Europe or in overseas markets, and inside Europe any of the smaller countries which did join the Common Market would have to give tariff preferences to German and French cars if Britain did not join. The effects of trying to shirk the challenge of the Volkswagen might well be worse for the British motor industry than those of accepting the need to meet German producers on their own grounds of standardisation of products and efficient servicing. It is also worth while noting that the total production of motor cars in Western Europe including Britain in 1955, was less than a third of that in the United States. In any industry where substantial economies would resuit from an increase of scale of production, Britain's relative costs would be increased by staying out of a Free Trade Area.

Another group of industries in which alarm has been expressed at the prospect of more competition is textiles. In 1954 Britain exported £284 million worth of textiles more than she imported: the ' net exports ' of the Schumann Plan Countries were £393 million, while the rest of Western Europe had ' net imports ' of over £89 million. Obviously the maintenance of Britain's net export position in textiles must depend chiefly on being able to provide overseas countries with their textile needs at prices as reasonable as those of other major exporters, and staying out of a European Free Trade area could not help with this, while as in the case of cars it would hinder British sales to European countries which did join.

The second fear about the impact of a free trade area concerns the effects of competing with people with lower standards of living than in Britain. Fears on this score cannot simply be dismissed on the theoretical grounds that, according to the law of comparative costs, absolute wage levels are irrelevant to the gains from trade available to any one country, since it is also agreed that the distribution of incomes can be affected by trading with countries with different relative factor-supplies. Adducing relevant facts on this issue is difficult because of the extreme elusiveness of information on relative factor prices in different countries (owing to differences of currencies, classification of trades, etc.). All that can be done without a special study is to give some indication of relative living standards of the populations of the four major Western European countries.

International comparisons of living standards are difficult to make precisely, but it is certainly true that consumption per head in Britain is higher than in Western Germany or France, and much higher than in Italy. Measuring at average European prices of 1950, in 1955 consumption per head was £270 in Britain, against £228 in France, £211 in Western Germany, and £118 in Italy. It is significant, however, that measured in the same way, consumption per head in Britain had increased since 1950 by only 8 per cent, compared to 17 per cent in Italy, 21 per cent in France, and 40 per cent in Western Germany: thus the relative difference in living standards has been narrowing.[1] Why this has happened is in turn shown by the fact that, on the

---

[1] It is noteworthy that a continuation of these trends for another 5 years would mean that it would not be Britain which needed to worry about competition by cheap labour; such a continuation is unlikely, however, since much of the German rate of increase must be attributed to post-war recovery.

average of the 6 years from 1950 to 1955, Western Germany invested slightly more per capita than Britain, though her consumption was only 71 per cent of the British level. It should also be noted that between 1950 and 1955 consumption per capita in Western Germany rose from 60 per cent to 78 per cent of that in Britain, and investment from 88 per cent to 112 per cent of the British figures; though there is no means of knowing how far this was due to delayed recovery from the war. Italy invested 52 per cent as much per capita as Britain in 1950–55, while consuming only 43 per cent as much, and France invested 90 per cent, while consuming 81 per cent as much per capita as Britain.

TABLE XXI

Rate of Growth of Investment plus Consumption in Table XX

Country	Percentage increase over previous year					Average of 1953–1955
	1951	1952	1953	1954	1955	
Great Britain ...	−2	−1	5	4	5	5
Western Germany ...	7	6	9	7	9	8
France	4	1	2	5	6	4
Italy	3	3	5	3	6	5

Source. As for Table XX.

While Britain's living standards are still higher than in most other European countries, her ability to maintain them depends not on protection from European competition, but on adequate investment and rises in productivity. Also, as Britain depends on overseas markets for essential supplies of foodstuffs and raw materials, it is there rather than at home that the main challenge of exports from more progressive countries must be met.

The remaining major danger in entering a Free Trade Area is that the removal of tariffs as a means of restricting imports from Europe might interfere with the attainment of full employment at home. This is because if British prices and wages became too high relative to other countries, or if the effort put into organising export markets fell too low because of the ease of selling at home, there might be no way of safeguarding the exchange reserves except by deflation. It is not only the Free Trade Area policy which involves this type of danger, of course; for tariffs are not at present a flexible means of restricting imports, since G.A.T.T. prevents Britain from increasing at will either her present tariffs or the degree of discrimination between Commonwealth suppliers and others, and exports can be as effectively restricted by excessive costs and prices as by other countries' tariffs. Freer trade would increase this type of danger however, especially as it would presumably be accompanied by either an explicit or a gentlemen's agreement that quantitative restrictions should be avoided as far as possible, and conversion to the new policy might involve short-run balance of payments problems which were quite serious, though spreading the process over 12 to 15 years would assist in making the necessary adjustments.

The acceptance of limitations on the right of each country to impose direct controls on imports would also tend to accentuate the difficulty of dealing with short-run balance of payments problems due to causes other than the change-over to a regime of lower intra-European tariffs. To get some indication of the possible magnitude of balance of payments difficulties due to these causes, it is interesting to examine the effects of the start of the European Trade Liberalisation programme on the balance of payments of various European countries, as shown in the early accounts of the European Payments Union. Western Germany started with a deficit of £130 million in the second half of 1950 and had to be helped by special credits to overcome this: later however Germany became a persistent creditor of the other E.P.U. countries, with a cumulative credit balance of £285 million by the end of 1953. Belgium, who started as a creditor, had a cumulative credit balance of £290 million by the end of 1953. Great Britain, on the other hand, started as a creditor, but developed an import surplus in 1951 which was partly responsible for her cumulative debit balance of £206 million by the end of 1953 (though this also reflects the results of the trade of the rest of the Sterling Area with E.P.U. countries).

It cannot be assumed that the creation of a free trade area will not involve fluctuations in the balance of payments at least as serious as these; though just as in the case of trade liberalisation, special arrangements could be made for the countries concerned to give each other credit. These might well include a reduction in the E.P.U. gold-payments fraction. If such arrangements were not made, it would imply that the deficit countries would have to try to cure their import surpluses by means of deflation (though the existence of time-lags might render even deflation ineffective in the very short run necessitated by inadequate exchange reserves). This makes it important to consider possible forms of insurance against short-run balance of payments difficulties.

In principle, there are two ways in which the problem of deficits in the balance of payments which might arise through a conversion to freer European trade could be solved. The first is that the monetary and fiscal systems of the countries concerned should be co-ordinated, so that investment and government spending would be expanded in 'surplus' countries and contracted in 'deficit' countries, to correct the balance. However, given independent systems of wage-bargaining in different countries—and in different industries within each country—and given stable exchange-rates, such a system would mean that the countries concerned were giving up the right to be as inflationary or deflationary as they themselves chose: this would involve governments at times in policies which were exceedingly unpopular, and might be difficult to reconcile with political independence. While no country is in any case free from all external influences on its wage system and investment policy—and for a country like Britain it is particularly necessary to behave sensibly about these things in a hard world, which does not feel it owes her a relatively luxurious living unless she can earn it—freer trade means a little less freedom to pursue independent full-employment

TABLE XXII

E.P.U. Balances of Selected Western European Countries

The cumulative balances are shown as a sum of the period figures and do not allow for initial balances, special payments, funding, or interest on accrued balances, and thus do not correspond to the actual, published E.P.U. balances. The figures below, however, give an idea of the order of magnitude of the payments problems which might arise.

(in £mn.)

Period		Great Britain		Western Germany		France		Italy		Belgium and Luxembourg	
		period	cumulative total	period	cumulative total	period	cumulative total	period	cumulative total	period	cumulative total
1950 2nd half	...	+170	+170	−132	−132	+76	+76	−11	−11	+2	+2
1951 1st half	...	+47	+217	+30	−102	−6	+70	0	−11	+82	+84
1951 2nd half	...	−385	−168	+113	+11	−141	−71	+80	+69	+131	+215
1952 1st half	...	−152	−320	+95	+106	−83	−154	−11	+58	+69	+284
1952 2nd half	...	+79	−241	+23	+129	−76	−230	−22	+36	+19	+303
1953 1st half	...	+53	−188	+70	+199	−73	−303	−57	−21	−14	+289
1953 2nd half	...	−18	−206	+85	+284	−34	−337	−33	−54	−1	+288

N.B.   The British figures include the balances of other Sterling Area countries (except Iceland) with E.P.U. countries.

Source.   E.C.E. Economic Survey of Europe in 1954, Table XXV, p. 217.

(or, in some countries, price stability) policies. That little may or may not be felt to outweigh the effects of improved efficiency through larger markets; this is for everybody concerned to decide.

There is however another possible alternative means of adjusting the balance of payments, and that is to agree on international investment by the surplus members of at least a share of their surpluses on current account. It is possible to think of several uses for these surpluses—though what follows cannot be treated as more than general suggestions, and the details would of course have to be agreed between all the countries concerned. There are several forms of investment which should prove acceptable in principle to all the members of a European Free Trade Area. First, there is the development of atomic power in the 'Eurotam' scheme: this is a project vital to all the European countries, and for which they will have to raise the capital somehow if it is adopted. A scheme by which the various countries would contribute investment quotas which would be reduced in years when they had payments deficits and increased when they had surpluses would mean that countries which in any one year wanted to save more than they could conveniently invest at home, and therefore had a balance of payments surplus, would be able to do this without inconveniencing their neighbours by draining off their gold and dollar reserves.

A second possible use for such funds would be in helping to provide the resources for urgently needed development projects. These could take the form of projects to help the most backward parts of the area, such as southern Italy, which is as poor relative to northern Italy as Italy herself is compared to Britain. Also, there are projects for investments of common interest to various countries, such as the proposed improvements in the navigation of the Moselle, which connects the French iron-fields of Lorraine with the German coal area of the Ruhr, and would also help the steel-producers of Luxembourg.

Finally, there is the possibility that the resources of a European Investment Fund could be used for investment in under-developed countries outside Europe, both to provide the supplies of raw materials which Europe needs, and to promote the general well-being of the people of these countries (such as India or Indonesia), in whose goodwill and progress Europeans have a common interest. Such uses could of course be channelled through United Nations' bodies, the Colombo Plan, or any other suitable agency: the European Fund would however allocate the contributions amongst its members in each particular year so that countries paid when it was most convenient to them.

In proposing to provide resources for development outside Europe, it is however necessary to remember that this can only be done if Western Europe as a whole has a balance of payments surplus with the rest of the world; for investment inside Europe this problem would not arise.

Whether Britain should join in a Free Trade Area with the proposed Common Market in Western Europe is a question which cannot be decided either on purely economic grounds, or by its effect on the economic interests of any one country; all this article has tried to do is to provide some of the facts, and point out some of their implications, to help in reaching a sensible decision. Though entry into a Free Trade Area has its dangers, so has being left out—for a people situated as we are in Britain, there is no policy which can avoid all possible dangers. Yet it appears to the writer that, provided that reasonable time for adjustment is allowed, as is in fact proposed, and provided that proper measures are taken to even out any dislocation in the balance of payments which occurs while we are converting to freer trade, joining in the scheme rather than staying out provides better hopes of progress both for Britain and for the other countries of Western Europe.

THE CRITERIA OF ECONOMIC ADVANTAGE

By HARRY G. JOHNSON

Until last year, British foreign economic policy was inclined to take a consistently negative and unfriendly attitude towards the successive moves in the direction of European economic integration which have led up to the scheme for enlarging the European Coal and Steel Community into a fully-fledged common market. The new enthusiasm for participation, like the uninterestedness which preceded it, probably owes more to political emotion than to economic calculation; at any rate, strong undertones of fear of German domination of Europe, dissatisfaction with the Commonwealth, and the revulsion from the Atlantic Alliance which prompted the Suez disaster, have been clearly detectable in the favourable reaction to the Government's scheme. Recognition of the political aspects of the question does not necessarily imply the need for judgment on political grounds, if only because political motivations and political consequences are not the same thing[1]; nor does it diminish the economic interest of the problem. What it does imply, however, is the need for exercising particular care in distinguishing between valid economic arguments and politically-appealing pseudo-arguments, and for attempting to assess the quantitative significance of the former. In this respect Mr. Black's introductory article implicitly accepts the popular terms of the debate much too readily, and despite its plethora of statistics provides little of the material required. This comment will therefore be concerned with a discussion of the economic criteria which should be applied in assessing the proposal; a corresponding quantitative exercise is called for but will not be provided here.

To begin with, something must be said about the general viewpoint that should be adopted in appraising economic policy proposals of this kind. The question of Britain's relationship with the proposed Common Market involves a choice between alternative long-run economic environments, and should be approached primarily from the standpoint of prospective long-run effects on potential real income or the productivity of national resources. Transitional problems, and problems arising from other aspects of economic policy, should be regarded as logically secondary matters, whose seriousness varies inversely with the long-run gain afforded by the chosen environment; they should, that is, be regarded more as obstacles to be overcome in, than as valid objections to, the establishment of the desirable environment.

This comment will accordingly concentrate on the calculation of long-run benefits, rather than on the discussion of transitional and incidental problems. It may be remarked in passing, however, that the objections to British participation in the Free Trade area discussed by Mr. Black all relate to the latter type of problem, and that his treatment of them is not

[1] In the writer's view, closer European political and economic co-operation is the natural long-run trend, as the growing importance of other continents increasingly emphasizes the common characteristics of, and reduces the apparent significance of differences between, European nations.

fully satisfactory from the point of view outlined above. In the first place, as will be argued below, it is not a ' danger ' but an essential source of gain from participation that certain existing British industries will be forced to contract; if participation is desirable, the problem is to predict which industries will contract and make arrangements to minimize the wastes entailed. Second, a reduction in the relative wages of workers in the better-off countries may be an incidental result of the improved efficiency made possible by the Free Trade area; if necessary it could be compensated by social policy. Third, abnegation of balance-of-payments restrictions on imports makes it more difficult, not to maintain full employment, but to combine full employment with a fixed exchange rate; acceptance of the exchange rate as a datum of analysis and not as a policy variable greatly exaggerates the balance-of-payments objection to any move towards freer trade, by precluding a rational discussion of policy objectives and benefits.[1]

The popular view of the long-run advantages of British participation in the proposed Free Trade area, which is reflected in Mr. Black's article, concentrates on the economies of scale made possible by a larger market; while recognizing the possibility of some gains accruing via the expansion of trade between members, it tends to regard the increased competition from European industry as a danger and a threat to British industry. It will be argued here, on the contrary, that the likelihood of economies of scale as such is extremely small, and that the main gains, though difficult to assess, are likely to be found precisely in the direction viewed with the most alarm, namely the replacement of British by European production of certain types of goods.[2]

There are several reasons for scepticism about the likely importance of gains from economies of scale through enlargement of the market via the creation of the Free Trade area.[3] One is that it is not at all obvious that an agglomeration of national markets, each with its own language, customs, and distribution methods, would offer the same opportunity for mass distribution as a homogeneous national market of the same size. Again, observation of the American market suggests that the mass consumer is a special consuming type, qualitatively different from a mass of consumers. As against these considerations, it can be argued that a great deal of selling is from producer to producer or producer to large-scale distributor, and in such transactions technical performance and cost play a more decisive role than in consumer sales.

[1] Oxford economists seem to have agreed on a conspiracy of silence in defence of the postwar dollar standard, recognizing only deflation or import controls as legitimate means of dealing with deficits.

[2] Sometimes increased competition is regarded as beneficial, on the assumption that it will *not* in the long run eliminate British firms. The benefit depends on whether the firms survive by improving efficiency, or by squeezing profits and/or wages, the latter being for the most part merely a distributional change. One version of this argument is that the larger market area will check the power of monopoly—clearly not a decisive argument since there are other ways of dealing with monopoly.

[3] For a reasoned analysis of possible gains, see Tibor Scitovsky, " Economies of Scale and European Integration ", *American Economic Review*, Vol. XLVI, No. 1, (March 1956).

In addition to the question as to how far the apparent enlargement of the market would be an effective enlargement promoting larger-scale production and distribution, there is a more important question as to how far there exist unexploited economies of scale which depend upon a larger market for their exploitation. It is extremely difficult to believe that British industry offers substantial potential savings in cost which cannot be exploited in a densely-populated market of 51 million people with a G.N.P. of £18 billion, especially when account is taken of the much larger markets abroad in which British industry, in spite of restrictions of various kinds, has been able to sell its products. What the Free Trade area offers is not escape from a strait-jacket of 51 million people, but a less restricted access than heretofore to part of the world market. And where there seems to be a *prima facie* possibility of substantial gains from economies of scale—the motor trade is the one generally agreed example—the question arises as to why these economies have not been exploited already, and how far the larger size of the Free Trade area by itself would stimulate exploitation.

These various considerations suggest that the economies of scale expected to be achieved by the Free Trade area may be largely illusory. Credence in them seems to be based on a superficial analogy with the United States, accepted because of its political appeal. That the analogy's appeal is political rather than economic, tends to be confirmed by the coupling in the argument with the United States of the Russian economy, which has been suddenly cast in a new and unexpected role—as an example of what can be done by free trade on a large enough scale.

The more rewarding direction in which to look for possible economic benefits from participation in the scheme is to the effects on Britain's real income of the consequent changes in the pattern of production, consumption, and trade—since the necessity of such changes can be inferred from the existence of substantial trade at current tariff levels. Here recent developments in the theory of international trade are highly relevant.[1] These developments have had the general effect of destroying any presumption that a limited move towards free trade will prove beneficial to the participants, while at the same time clarifying the sources of benefit and loss and the nature of the calculations that need to be made in assessing any particular scheme.

The reason why there is no clear answer in principle to the question of which of the three alternatives—Common Market, Free Trade area, non-participation—is preferable, is that all three, like the present framework of British trade, are characterized by discrimination both between domestic British producers and foreign producers and between groups of foreign producers, and choice between them is a choice between non-optimum environments, for which theory provides no universally valid principle.[2]

[1] *Cf.* in particular J. E. Meade, *The Theory of Customs Unions.*
[2] *Cf.* R. G. Lipsey and K. Lancaster, ' The General Theory of Second Best ', *Review of Economic Studies*, Vol. XXIV No. 1 (October, 1955).

Comparison of the alternatives requires detailed analysis of the consequences for real income of the accompanying shifts in the trade pattern; it cannot rest on consideration of changes in the aggregate volume of trade only, since discrimination implies that some kinds of trade are more valuable than others.

The effects of any change in a country's trade policy on its economic welfare can be conveniently analysed under three heads : production effects, consumption effects, and terms of trade effects.[1] The change may shift production of the things the country consumes to a more efficient or to a less efficient source of production; it may shift consumption towards a more or a less satisfactory pattern; and it may improve or worsen the country's terms of trade, by shifting demand towards or away from the country's goods.[2] The terms of trade effects of the three alternatives will be considered first, since the analysis of them is familiar.

Non-participation in the Common Market would probably involve significant adverse terms of trade effects, owing to the discrimination against British goods in favour of European competitors in the European market; a rough maximum measure of the loss involved would be the extent to which export prices would have to be reduced to counteract this discrimination and retain present sales, which would depend on the level of the common Market tariff. The adverse effect would be partly offset by the effect of the diversion of members' production and consumption towards the common market in reducing competition with British goods elsewhere. For the same reason full membership would tend to mean improved terms of trade with non-members, though this might be more than offset by retaliatory reductions in preferences enjoyed under Imperial Preference, while the effects on terms of trade with other members would depend on the net effects on reciprocal demands of the elimination of mutual tariffs. The Free Trade area, which seeks to avoid provoking loss of preferential treatment by retaining discrimination in favour of members of the preferential system as against other non-Europeans and by exempting ' food, drink and tobacco ', would seem to offer the most favourable terms of trade effects, to an extent depending on how far the advantages of the Imperial Preference system can be retained.[3] Perhaps the safest course, however, would be not to place too much emphasis

[1] See the study by Dr. W. M. Corden, ' The Calculation of the Cost of Protection ', forthcoming in the *Economic Record*, for an application of these concepts to the theory of tariffs.

[2] The complication that terms of trade effects will induce production and consumption shifts, while production and consumption effects may be reflected in terms of trade changes, will be ignored in what follows.

[3] The assumption that the concessions mentioned will satisfy the other members of the Imperial Preference system may be ill-founded; Canada is already dissatisfied with the system, and other industrializing members may become increasingly dissatisfied with the discrimination against their manufactures in the British market inherent in the Free Trade area scheme. Nor is the added promise of a larger supply of development capital very convincing. On the other hand, the average margin of preference Britain now enjoys is relatively small, and loss of it may not be too serious. Sir Donald Macdougall and Rosemary Hutt (" Imperial Preference : A Quantative Analysis ", *Economic Journal*, Vol. LXIV, No. 254, June 1954) estimated the average preference margin on U.K. trade with the Commonwealth at only 6 per cent in either direction.

on terms of trade effects, since they depend so heavily on the reactions of other countries' trade policies, as well as other complex reactions.

The analysis of both production and consumption effects centres on the fact that import duties create a divergence between the real costs of imports to the country in terms of exports, and their apparent costs (and marginal values) to residents,[1] a divergence measurable at the margin by the rate of tariff actually imposed, or that equivalent to the degree of quantitative restriction. With rates and restrictions differentiated by commodity and origin, the divergence between real cost and apparent cost (value) also differs. It follows that a re-allocation of a given total expenditure due to some change in one or more tariffs might either increase or decrease real income, depending on whether it tended to increase or decrease the surplus of value over real cost (the consumption effect). Similarly, such a tariff change might either increase or decrease the real cost of a given amount of consumption, depending on whether it shifted production of the goods consumed towards higher or lower-cost sources (the production effect).

In the case of tariff reductions, the consumption effect is more likely to be favourable, the higher the initial and final levels of the tariffs which are reduced, relative to the levels of the unchanged tariffs, and the more consumption of the imports affected is increased at the expense of domestic rather than other imported commodities. The production effect may take either of two forms: a shift from domestic to foreign sources of supply, which is necessarily favourable, and a shift from one foreign source to another, which is favourable or unfavourable according to whether the new source of supply would have been chosen over the old at a tariff rate the same for both, or not, the loss in the latter case varying with the tariff differential necessary to induce the shift.

Application of the analysis of production and consumption effects, of which the foregoing is merely a brief sketch, to a calculation of the potential net benefit from participation in the Free Trade area would obviously require a great deal of information on existing tariff levels, demand functions, and production possibilities in Britain and elsewhere, since what is relevant is not the volume and composition of existing trade but the changes that would occur as a consequence of the Free Trade area. For this purpose, figures on domestic production and sources of imports in the different categories, together with tariff levels, would be more suggestive than export figures, which bear more on the possible consequences of non-participation or loss of Imperial Preference.

As the scheme has been described so far, and given the high levels of tariffs and other protection accorded British manufacturing production in the home market and existing discriminations favouring European over American goods, it would seem that the most important consump-

---

[1] It must be emphasized that terms of trade effects are ignored in what follows—as are other potential causes of divergence between real and money domestic costs, which are assumed to be taken care of by appropriate policies.

tion and production shifts for Britain are likely to be from British to European and from American to European products, the former shifts involving substantial gains and the latter (unless there is a very strong terms of trade effect) substantial losses. Since consumption shifts are difficult to distinguish from production shifts, owing to the difficulty of defining products, and since in any case both types of shift entail a shift in the location of production of goods consumed in Britain, the balance of advantage can be said to depend on the relative magnitude of the gains from replacement of British by European production, and the losses by replacement of American by European production, in British consumption. This criterion implies, as was remarked at the beginning of this comment, that the fears of disturbance expressed by certain well-protected British industries such as motors and textiles are pointers to probable advantages rather than the reverse. But whether the economic advantages outweigh the disadvantages, and if so by how much, is a question whose answer could only be approached by a detailed calculation.

LIBERALIZATION OR CONSTRUCTIVE ORGANIZATION

OR: THE HAIR OF THE DOG THAT BIT

By T. BALOGH

I

(1) In the period 1944–50 one of the most acute disagreements about British economic policy was on the question of 'regional blocs'. The traditional 'free(r) trade' view was that the discriminating policies which such organisation implied—either monetary or commercial—were contrary to the national interest, since they reduced productivity. As against this a few authors, including Sir Hubert Henderson, pointed out that the need for large-scale readjustment would be impeded by the restoration of free markets, and, in addition, that the dynamism of the U.S. economy was likely to recreate periodically the need for such large-scale adjustment. Only a large regional bloc comprising at least the Sterling Area and possibly Western Europe and its dependencies would offer a chance of creating the conditions for large productive units to arise spontaneously which would be capable of meeting U.S. competition on equal terms. I still hold the view that the emergence of such a regional economic bloc is essential if Europe is to meet the threat implied in the rise of the two giant continental economic systems.

(2) After the 1947 crisis the U.S.A. ceased to press for the implementation of the universalist solution embodied in the Bretton Woods Agreements. Veering to the other extreme it promoted and granted aid under the aegis of O.E.E.C. for a discriminatory common planning of Western European investment. As production was still at a low ebb such a co-ordination of investment could have been made effective without actually bankrupting existing firms. Britain was then in a dominant position in Western Europe such as she had not enjoyed since the late 1880's. She would therefore have been the main spontaneous beneficiary of the creation of such a bloc. It would, of course, have been morally and politically imperative to channel investment towards the poorer members of the new unit. Nevertheless there can be little doubt that if Britain had acted at that time, she could hardly have failed to strengthen both her relative and absolute position.

(3) This conception foundered on the determination of the Treasury and the Bank of England to return towards the ' normality ' of the free price mechanism by as rapid a decontrol as possible. The O.E.E.C mechanism was never used to plan for Europe just as the Sterling Area was not organically developed. The consequence was a series of post-war economic and balance of payments crises. This in turn enforced—as all direct controls were disappearing—an increasing reliance upon dear money and the credit squeeze to buttress the short-run position of the pound. But, as an expansion of investment and an acceleration of the increase of productivity is the sole

37

way of restoring balance without having to sacrifice economic progress, this policy in the longer run is suicidal.

(4) Having resisted common European and Commonwealth planning at a time when Britain was economically dominant in Europe it is now proposed to join a Western European economic bloc on the basis of free trade. Mr. Black's paper analyses the various quantitative aspects of the proposed union and there is no need to go over that ground. In this paper I shall confine myself to showing:

(a) that the rapid development of Germany has created a problem for the Western European area superficially similar to, but basically more dangerous than, the dollar problem, i.e. the impact of a higher dynamism within a region on the rest of the system. In so far as the German economy is similar to ours and does not create special problems for primary producers, its impact on us is much greater and will manifest itself in a steady pressure on our terms and balance of trade;

(b) that our bargaining power in this matter is not as weak as has been suggested by a misreading of relevant statistics;

(c) that that bargaining power should be used, not indeed to prevent the formation of a European Bloc, but to secure its transformation into a positive organ of expansionist planning;

(d) that this implies, first the loosening of the European Payments Union, preferably by creating a common Central Bank; secondly the channelling of investment towards the areas of slower growth in order to achieve balance by expansion and not by deflation;

(e) that the danger for Britain is of an imposed deflation—rather than of inflation, and the suggestion that this could be avoided by adopting a floating rate of exchange is mistaken; it would instead ruin Britain's capacity to remain the banker of the Sterling Area and largely vitiate the purported aim of the ' Free Trade Area '.

II

(5) The basic reason for the relative weakness of Britain was, and remains, the failure to invest.[1] The essential facts are simple : in most of the important countries of the proposed free trade area, except Germany, gross investment is well below 20 per cent of the national income, with net investment around 10 per cent.[2] In Germany the ratio of gross investment to gross national income was around 28 per cent and net investment to net national income 15 per cent, almost twice as high as the corresponding British figure for 1955. Thus German investment in manufacturing industry in absolute terms rose above the British level from RM 6.0 b. in 1950 to RM 10.0 b. in 1955 as against from £500 m. to £ 890 m., and investment in metal industry

[1] I have analysed this problem elsewhere (*Review of Economics and Statistics*, 1957).

[2] Norway, Finland, Austria and Switzerland achieved about the same ratio of investment as Germany.

(which increased from 32 per cent of the total in 1950 to 56 per cent in 1955, while ours rose only from 36 to 42 per cent) increased far above it. Germany overhauled Britain in the output of steel, cement, bricks, motor-cars, machine tools and other vital products. Moreover, German productivity in the past three years has been increasing at the rate of over 6 per cent and this increase has not radically slackened yet. It permitted an increase in German money wages of roughly 4 per cent without a perceptible increase in German living costs (4 per cent since 1954); thus German real wages rose at nearly the same rate. In contrast to this, British money wages rose 6 per cent in the same period, a large part of it being wiped out by a rise in prices which amounted to over 10 per cent.

It is not surprising, therefore, that Britain's relative competitive power declined; German exports rose from $2.0 billion in 1950 to $6.5 billion in 1955 while British expanded only from $6.3 billion to $8.5 billion. The discrepancy in the expansion in the field of durable consumer goods was even more marked: German exports in the last two years increased by 50 per cent: ours remain practically unchanged. German monetary reserves— which were practically non-existent even as late as 1950—at almost $4 billion are now the second largest in the non-Soviet world and more than 50 per cent above ours. This tremendous hoard was accumulated despite the millions paid out by Germany in reparations, repatriation of claims and assets, foreign loans and premature repayment of debt.

The problem raised by the more rapid growth of the German economy cannot be met, of course, simply by maintaining or increasing our own protectionism. It is, like the problem of America on the larger canvas of the whole non-Soviet orbit, a *cumulative* problem which cannot be met by *once-for-all* measures. Unless the basic British situation is remedied there can be no hope of being able to maintain an increase in the British standard of life commensurate with the expectations which have been raised. The problem which has to be discussed in this context is whether the establishment of a ' free trade area' will or will not increase the difficulties, which are in any case very great, in the way of a rapid acceleration of British investment. To that problem we shall now turn.

(6) The whole of our post-war history has been dominated by our balance of payments problem. Despite assertions to the contrary, every wave of liberalisation has been followed by a severe balance of payments crisis which entailed severe retrenchment. Retrenchment and deflation, unfortunately, can hardly fail to depress investment, and thus it could be argued that liberalisation has not merely not eased our basic problems but it has made them insoluble since it prevented attempts at transforming Britain from a low into a high investment country. So long as this remains unchanged it is inconceivable for Britain to hold her own either in Europe or in third markets with the increasing competitive power of Germany.

(i) The establishment of a Free Trade Area would tend to increase our imports. No doubt, the liberalisation will also stimulate our exports.

But Britain is a relatively high tariff area and it is by no means certain that the relaxation of tariffs all round would stimulate our exports as much as it would stimulate imports. A similar (though not identical) problem is that the freeing of European non-agricultural trade from tariffs is likely to increase the swings in the balance of payments. Any increase in the swing however, would, with the gold reserves as low as they are, entail a harsher reaction at home than would be needed with a smaller relative volume of trade.

(*ii*) A relaxation of all control over imports from the Free Trade Area would in the end necessarily entail a relaxation of discrimination against dollar countries. Dollar imports in the most important countries of the prospective Free Trade Area are already largely decontrolled and, if for no other reason than the difficulty in coping with re-exports, this would entail a progressive adaptation of our liberalisation to that of the least restrictive important foreign country in the Free Trade Area. Otherwise, the re-exportation by these countries into Britain of dollar supplies would represent the reverse of our supplying dollar raw materials against sterling payments to the Continent. It will obviously weaken the situation of the bloc as a whole against the dollar and, unless E.P.U. is adjusted, weaken our position *vis-à-vis* the Free Trade Area.

(*iii*) In this connection it should be noted that according to the continental plans the reimposition of import controls, even in accordance with G.A.T.T., will be prohibited. But even if they were not, it would be very difficult to impose them so as to ensure that members of the Commonwealth should not be treated worse than the members of the Free Trade Area, and at the same time that the Free Trade Area should not treat us worse than it treats any other member. If, in addition, the difficulties are taken into account which any discrimination in favour of these two groups will entail in our relations with the United States and Canada, the conclusion is hardly escapable that the establishment of a Free Trade Area will render the framing of a sensible commercial policy more difficult.

(*iv*) It should be noted that liberalisation all round has not always worked in our favour. While this should not come as a surprise to those who realise the importance of a relative increase in productivity for the balance of payments, it is a fact which has been studiously neglected. Exports to the Dollar Area have increased by more than a third since 1950, while the liberalisation of imports into Europe has only had the result of increasing our exports by 15 per cent. Now there is no doubt that the German problem will present a very much harsher choice to Britain. If our balance of payments cannot be influenced by any direct means we shall have to fall back on either a depreciation of sterling or an even sharper use of bank rate, or on increasing budgetary surpluses.

(*v*) I shall deal with fluctuating rates of exchange presently. In this context I merely wish to point out that an increase in interest rates has a devastating effect on the assets of the poorer Sterling Area members' investment at long term and will stimulate repatriation of their reserves at least as fast as the assets mature, *i.e.* stimulate an indefinite drain on sterling. This will react on the London monetary position and reinforce the demand for still higher rates of interest.[1]

(*vi*) Dear money, even if reinforced by direct credit control, has only a limited effect on investment or even on stocks, so long as full employment is maintained. Its effect is counteracted by an appropriate shift in the distribution of income. At the same time, an atmosphere created by a continuous upward trend of interest rates is not one in which a rapid expansion of investment is probable. I feel, therefore, that a policy which excludes direct control of the balance of payments will under these conditions steadily force us into direct nationalisation, since tax measures combined with a budget surplus, which would be an alternative, would also discourage investment unless they were to fall more heavily on the poorer classes.

(7) It could be argued, of course, that even if these dangers were considerable the danger of remaining outside the Free Trade Area would be much greater. Mr. Black's figures represent an eloquent testimony to the force of this argument.

Two points need to be made in this context:

(*a*) Even if we assume the Common Market of the Six will come into being in any case, the decision of Britain to join the new organisation is, if not the decisive one, at least a very important factor determining whether a larger Free Trade Area will come into being. But only just over half of our total exports and imports to O.E.E.C. countries are in our trade with the Common Market.[2] Thus our refusal to join in the Free Trade Area would be a factor of great importance to all European countries. This means that our bargaining position is by no means a weak one. It is strengthened by the fact that Britain has a large net deficit with both the Common Market Area (£106m. in 1955) and the O.E.E.C. territory as a whole (£152m. in 1955). The fact that this import surplus is derived from a much larger import surplus (£309m.) in food, beverages and tobacco and basic materials, and a net export surplus in other classes of goods (especially manufactures), increases this bargaining power at present, since Britain remains practically the only market for certain higher value types of agricultural produce. In the longer run, when German consumption, and her imports of these classes

---

[1] The blocking of the Egyptian sterling balances has already weakened confidence in London as an international banking centre, from which it will find it difficult to recover in any case. Any further inimical measure against creditors would be fatal.

[2] And as M. Mendes-France's speech to the French Assembly shows (*Manchester Guardian*, 15 January, 1957), Britain's attitude might well be decisive even in the formation of the Common Market itself.

of goods, will increase, this bargaining power might weaken. But at the moment it is still strong.[1]

It is further increased by the fact that the European export surplus to this country is used by Europe to offset her large adverse balance of payments with the tropics, the overseas food and raw material suppliers, and, above all, America. Part at least of Britain's dollar problem has been caused by the steady re-export of dollar commodities against sterling payments to the Continent of Europe whose dollar problem has been solved, so to say, on our backs. The fact that London reaped a trifling commission[2] out of this steady drain of our economic strength does not detract from the importance of this service to the continent.

We could, therefore, hope to bargain very effectively with Europe when it comes to establishing a common tariff against our exports to Europe. This, added to the consideration that the new tariff area is hardly likely to be a high tariff area, very much weakens the argument that our exclusion would be fatal.

This does not mean that we should use our bargaining power to wreck the scheme or to contract out at least cost to ourselves. It does mean that we can and should insist on a modification of the scheme which would render it less risky and more hopeful for a full development of European productivity and competitive power.

(b) The second point concerns British relations with the Sterling Area. It is, to say the least, a curious fact that the very people who have always minimised the advantage to Britain of the existence of the preferential treatment of our exports in the Sterling Area and in E.P.U. through the existence of discrimination against dollar exports in E.P.U. or against both dollar and European exports in the Sterling Area, should suddenly see a deadly threat to our exports to Europe if preference is given to Germany or France by the rest by abolishing tariffs.

Yet it is unlikely that the tariffs in the common market will be much higher than in its low-tariff components, i.e. Germany or Benelux. This would mean the institution of, say, 20 per cent on the average by the rest of the area. The policy of liberalisation has meant the loss of a very much higher preference in the Sterling Area against Germany and the U.S. or against U.S. exports in the E.P.U. area. Yet advocates of free trade not only tolerated the systematic attack on our competitive position in the Sterling Area implied in the policy of liberalisation, but positively initiated and encouraged it. They fell into the illogical attitude of some American economists who favour 100 per cent preference yet oppose anything less drastic and thus (from the same misguided[3] theoretical point of view) less damaging.

No doubt, if present policies continued, the Sterling Area will be doomed

---

[1] The importance of this factor was demonstrated in the 1930's. Conversely, in the immediate post-war period this shortage of food, etc., increased the bargaining power of the producers.

[2] This fact might to some extent explain the steady support of the City for the policy of ' convertibility '.   [3] Cf., e.g., J. Viner, *Customs Union.*

to dissolution. But any measure which would reverse this trend could still secure important advantages for our exports in an area which takes more than 50 per cent of our exports and provides as much of our imports. Yet any measure which opens the British market to European competition necessarily weakens the coherence of the Sterling Area. It makes any special concession which we could make to Sterling Area purchases, e.g. through bulk purchase agreements, less possible, as such agreements could render our producers less competitive than those in other parts of Western Europe with free access to our markets. Conversely, our ceasing to grant preferential treatment to Sterling Area producers will render Sterling Area countries less willing to grant us a privileged position as against, say, Japanese or German or even American competition. This process has gone some way since we discontinued bulk purchase agreements, etc., to the Sterling Area producers.[1] This has impoverished primary producers and our exports equally suffered by cheaper competitors. If the Free Trade Area comes into being, manufacturers from the Commonwealth will suffer from the suppression of their preferences. In some cases European producers will be preferred by a complete suppression of all tariffs while Commonwealth supplies remain subject to duty. Thus the net immediate effect on our production of the entry into a Free Trade Area must be measured

(*a*) by the increase in our exports which would not have occurred had we not become members, *minus* the excess of imports, due to the same cause;

(*b*) the relative decline in our exports to the Sterling Area due to the same cause;

(*c*) the increase in dollar imports which has to be tolerated as a result of our entering an organisation less discriminating against the U.S.

It is not at all certain whether this immediate gain would be positive.

(8) It can be argued, however, that even if there is no immediate gain in the long run, the increase in productivity of all members of the new Common Market, and/or Free Trade Area, would more than offset all losses or other considerations. The Free Trade Area would provide a large enough market to increase the efficiency of European industries by rationalising production. I do not wish to press the point that Britain is already (at any rate so far as most industries are concerned) a sufficiently large market to provide outlets for optimum-sized productive units. There is no doubt that the oligopolistic tendency which limits rationalisation and tends to bring about quality differentiation has very much increased the minimum size of the market in which (despite the prevalence of oligopoly) units could be expected to arise spontaneously of a size capable of meeting American, and later Russian, competition on equal terms. I wonder, however, whether the merely negative act of opening national markets will be sufficient to achieve this end. We have been asked to believe that a whiff of the grapeshot of competition would

[1] *Cf.* Below (8).

be healthy for everybody. But has it worked out that way? It is interesting to observe that our exports to America have increased relatively more than those to the O.E.E.C. countries, even though trade with O.E.E.C. was liberalised more than that with America. Nor did the liberalisation in the Sterling Area seem to have brought about the regeneration which was hoped for. We lost trade to outside competitors in the Sterling Area, and Sterling Area producers lost markets in Britain.[1]

In the end, there has been ever since liberalisation a tightening of the capital market, only temporarily interrupted by the windfall improvement in the terms of trade in 1953. Is it likely that in conditions of dear money and harshness, uncertainty and violent competition with a better situated Germany, British investment will expand so as to create large-scale industries in Britain which are needed if Britain is not to be submerged by Germany within and without the free market? ' European ' production might well ' benefit ' with *Britain* suffering *absolute decline*. After all Naples joined Milan in a free market in 1860, and the merger wrought nothing in 100 years but destruction to her industries.

(9) This does not mean that we should oppose joining a Western European Organisation. But it does mean that we should be foolish if we joined without very special safeguards for our freedom of action in certain circumstances, and without seeing to it that the new Organisation will permit an expansionist solution of our problems, including the problem of maintaining the Sterling Area. Before I discuss what I would regard as the minimum safeguards for Britain, I must dispose of two problems which are closely connected with it.

(10) The first concerns the adoption of a fluctuating exchange rate. Some writers accept that a problem of short-term readjustment exists, which might be sharpened in extent by, and vitiate the beneficial long-run effects of, the ' New Deal for Europe ', but they maintain that permitting sterling to ' float ' freely would solve all these problems *automatically in an expansionist sense*. Nothing could, in my opinion, be further from the truth. Unless our inferiority in investment is cured, or our Trade Unions suddenly lose their bargaining power, a floating exchange would mean an exchange floating steadily downwards. As German relative competitive power increased, sterling would be under constant pressure. Two consequences follow:

(a) In the first place, an anticipated downward trend in the pound would render rationalisation through standardisation and mechanisation in our export industry unnecessary—*the ' readjustment ' would take the shape of a change in relative real wages, in the case of devaluation in an appropriate cut*. True enough, after a time it would result in a futile struggle for higher money wages[2] and lead to a repetition of the vicious circle of depreciation.

---

[1] The fact that Australia, India and some other countries are continuing or beginning their industrialisation does not detract from the fact that they are still more complementary to Britain, and are likely to remain so, than any of the countries of the proposed European union.

[2] *Cf.* Mr. Dow's brilliant analysis of the interrelation of import prices and cost inflation. *Oxford Economic Papers*, October, 1956.

But in the meanwhile precious time for a basic readjustment would have have been wasted. Devaluation or a floating pound, like tariffs, does not deal with the fundamental weakness. To deal with that weakness, and at the same time to increase overall productivity in Britain and in Europe, *a grosso modo* reorganisation of the productive structure is required. Fluctuating exchange rates (if effective at all) bring about *small* readjustments, shifting the limit of what is and what is not exported (and imported). They prevent the benefits due to productive reorganisation, the pretended reason for accepting the ' Free Trade Area ', from ever being achieved. The proposal is a flagrant example of the muddle resulting from the superimposition of a naive monetary theory on an equally naive ' real cost 'theory without attempting to fuse the two through applying a Keynesian approach to the problem.

(*b*) In the second place any anticipated depreciation of the pound would certainly ruin the country. Britain is a large-scale debtor, and the slightest suspicion that a fixed rate is not going to be defended will bring about a liquidation of foreign reserves in London. The depreciation through dear money of the assets which the Sterling Area countries (often compulsorily) had to invest in these reserves has already severely shaken confidence.[1] A policy which at least makes their further depreciation in terms of real value likely would destroy what is left. Thus a floating pound does not represent adequate safeguards for Britain.

(11) The second problem is raised by those who hope to safeguard the future of this country by negative safeguards, *i.e.* by retaining the right of imposing quantitative import and also exchange controls. As far as the latter the concerned they should raise not much difficulty, though an anticipated tightening is apt to induce the feared measure. But they are (in so far as they concern only capital movements) at least not at variance with the essential aim of the policy which is to obtain economies of large-scale production.

The possibility of re-imposing quantitative controls, however, is a different matter altogether. *If* import quotas are permissible no-one would take the risk of planning investment on a scale which needs the whole of the area for profitable operation. Thus we must conclude that any negative safeguards must be framed to become operative only after every effort to promote an expansionist solution to the balance of payments problem has failed. Otherwise the Free Trade Area scheme will only create uncertainty without (in a number of cases at least) contributing anything favourable to European revival and increase in productivity. Thus *some* limitation on sovereignty will have to be accepted. An entry into the Free Trade Area, if it is to have any favourable impact on productivity, must be non-reversible, otherwise no-one will invest in rationalising production. This means, however, that safeguards to protect national economies from the impact of intra-Free Trade Area competition must be very carefully planned. For this reason it is essential to secure positive safeguards that the re-imposition of controls will not become necessary. Yet in the Ministerial speeches con-

[1] *Cf.* above, p. 43, para. *v*

cerning our entry into Western Europe nothing was said about this vital matter.[1] This omission is so strange that it led some observers[2] to surmise that the surge of support for the Free Trade Area scheme in Britain can only be explained by the wish to preclude any Government in Britain from being able to restore direct planning and controls. The explicit prohibitions and implicit inhibitions of the scheme would be sufficient to guarantee a mainten-ance of the present status of economic 'freedom'. It is probable that this speculation is without real foundation. What is more likely (but not at all less dangerous) is that the authorities still do not realise the nature of the complex problems created by the faster growth of Germany and cling to the futile hopes of a simple-minded theory of the benefits of free trade. The profit motive of financial circles is a further, hardly less important, reason for the continued *malaise* of British policy. It is sometimes argued that it is inflationism rather than deflation which has to be guarded against. Con-temporary history does not bear out this view. In all Western countries the rise in the cost of living has become the most potent weapon to fight the Government. Both in Britain and in U.S. it was a decisive reason for the fall of administrations which had been exceptionally successful in maintaining employment and increasing real income. On the other hand persistent export surplus areas—especially Germany and the United States—have in the last five years pursued monetary policies which in the pre-1914 days of the undiluted gold standard would have been thought more appropriate for countries in heavy deficit. The result was to slow down output everywhere in the West—much to the detriment of our capacity to meet the Soviet challenge.

(12) What, then, are the safeguards which we should strive for?

(*a*) The expansionist solution of intra-European balance of payments difficulties has a short- and long-term requirement:

(*i*) The E.P.U. scheme must be reformed so as to decrease the likelihood of intra-European debit balances necessitating harsh deflationary action in any important country. Ideally, an E.P.U. Central Bank should be established which could at discretion discount bills for the debtor central bank in case of need. Alternatively, a much smaller rate of intra-European gold payments should be reintroduced with wider credit swings, instead of the present uniform gold percentage of 75 per cent of the monthly balance. It is obvious, however, that debtor governments cannot contemplate accumulating deficits to an unlimited extent. The causes of the unbalance must be tackled at their source. In order to facilitate this:

(*ii*) an investment board should be formed with borrowing powers (very much like the Coal and Steel Community) which would help debtor areas by positive investment projects. This would not only wipe out

---

[1] Labour policy statements were not quite explicit on this point either.
[2] *Cf. The Spectator*, Nov. 1956.

deficits but also would increase capacity where it is most needed and thus readjust the basic competitive position of the member countries and achieve the basic requirements for long-term equilibrium. Incidentally, the fact that such an investment board is established would powerfully counteract the increase in risk of intra-European investment to which liberalisation would inevitably lead.[1]

(b) There should be a careful definition of permissible re-exports to avoid the danger of being forced to liberalise against dollars.

(c) The member countries should retain the right of subsidising key industries as under G.A.T.T.

(d) Member countries should be permitted to maintain exchange control against panic flights of capital.

(e) Member countries, in addition, should be able to take fiscal measures to influence investment both so far as the total volume and its direction are concerned.

(f) The British Government must retain the right of maintaining more intimate connections with the Sterling Area apart from imperial preference. This in turn involves:

(i) the right to reintroduce bulk buying of foodstuffs and raw materials and to place long-term contracts; and

(ii) the working out of reciprocal trade agreements on the basis of increased British investment in the Sterling Area and the colonies. Without these the cohesion of the Sterling Area, which represents a preferential area of far greater importance than the Free Trade Area could conceivably be, would be jeopardised.

(g) Finally, *and only in case these more basic means of maintaining a dynamic equilibrium should fail through lack of co-operation,* and with severe safeguards against vexatious restrictions, member countries should be able to enforce quantitative restrictions for balance of payments purposes discriminating against a persistent surplus country by common consent.

A positive proposal framed in these terms would transform the present plan, which is fraught with danger for all areas of slower progress than Germany, into a forward-looking plan of equalising prosperity through expansion rather than sharing misery through deflation.

---

[1] It should be noted that the attempt of O.E.E.C. to co-ordinate investment in Europe in this sense failed. This should not, however, be quoted as a case against trying again.

The attempt failed (despite some American pressure in its favour) because none of the participating countries believed that it would benefit. They should by now be wiser if sadder by the experiences since 1950.

COMMON MARKET IN PERSPECTIVE

By R. F. HARROD

The economic effects of a European common market may be expected to be slow working. The plan itself envisages the dismantling of tariff barriers as gradual, and there may be hold-ups on the road. Furthermore, where competition is imperfect, we do not expect the opening of a market opportunity to yield its full dividend for a number of years. The need to get political decisions has caused leaders recommending the common market to over dramatise its probable effects. This does not imply that they are not giving a true bill. Cumulative effects over a long period may be of the utmost importance. The fact that they are likely to come but slowly does not in the least derogate from this.

Furthermore, some effects are likely to come quickly, namely, political effects. The advance by stages to a free trade area will involve much closer mutual consultation, not only in regard to technical matters relating to tariff adjustments, but also in regard to wider questions of economic policy. The offer of Marshall Aid created the O.E.E.C., which was a first landmark in the advance by the member countries towards greater mutual concern with each others' economic progress. The decision to have a common market would be an even more important landmark, and would quickly bring the countries closer together politically.

The over dramatisation, or rather I should say the telescoping, of the economic benefits likely to flow from the common market has its reverse effect also. If it can inspire enthusiasm, it may also inspire fear. If it is to bring large, quick benefits, this implies large adjustments ; and vested interests may quail. No doubt there will be hardships. These are of the essence of the scheme. Its main purpose is to get larger scale operation and longer production lines. This means more specialisation, and the elimination or reduction of output in lines in which each country is at a comparative disadvantage. But the adjustment is less painful if carried out in a context of expanding total output and demand, such as we hope will be realised in the next dozen years, whether there is a common market or not.

It might be of interest to illustrate this by a crude statistical exercise. In the 7 years from 1948 to 1955 British manufacturing output rose by 42 per cent. (Continental output showed similar increases). This was a rise of about 5 per cent a year. We should deflate this figure for the increase in the number employed in manufacturing, since no similar increase is likely to occur in the years ahead. This gives an increase of about 3.3 per cent a year per head. It would be an increase of about 50 per cent over a 12 year period. It is only at the end of 12 years that the system of free trade will be operating in full force, at earliest. The supposed increase of output of 50 per cent makes no allowance for such gains as may be registered owing to the coming into force of the common market itself, nor such speedier progress as may result from the higher level of investment recently realised in these countries.

In 1955 British manufacturing output was recorded as being worth £6,471 million. It is suggested that by the end of 12 years we may expect this to have risen by £3,240 million (at constant prices). Of this amount we may suppose, by simple extrapolation, that £1,440 million worth are required to buy more imports from non-O.E.E.C. countries. This leaves a residue of £1,800 million for sale to ourselves and to the other O.E.E.C. countries. This total includes, of course, capital goods and defence equipment as well as consumer goods. Let us suppose, no doubt by a heroic assumption, that from now onwards British producers regarded the whole of the ' common market' as their domestic market, and were able to sell to the various regions of the market in equal proportion to their buying power. This would mean a sale of £1,350 million worth of goods to the continental countries and only £450 million in Britain. By reciprocity, we should suppose a purchase of an additional £1,350 million worth of goods from the continent of Europe. This, be it noted, is allowing for British imports from non-O.E.E.C. countries to increase in line with the growth of British national income, *viz.* by £1,440 million at 1955 prices.

Such a development would involve a vast increase of intra-European trade. British exports to the other O.E.E.C. countries amounted to £760 million in 1955. Thus the supposition would involve almost trebling the trade. The object of this exercise has been to note that this terrific increase in trade could arise out of the mere expansion in demand to be expected in the next 12 years, not allowing for any possible increase in efficiency and consequential extra increase in demand that might be due to the common market itself. On this basis we could have a huge development of trade, even though British industry continued to supply *all the goods to the home market that it now supplies* and £450 million worth in addition. Such a transaction could be represented as being painless to existing vested interests. One could say to them, ' Look, you are selling just as much in the domestic market, and precisely the same goods, as you sold before all this thing started, and £450 million worth of goods in addition. What have you to complain of? It is only in regard to the expansion of sales that you might have had that you have been undercut by foreigners, but some of you have been able to achieve an expansion of equivalent value by the opening of the continental markets '. The gain from this arrangement would have flowed from the fact that the £1,350 million worth of goods supposed to be channelled into the continental market would not be a fair sample of goods now produced, but would be concentrated on the lines in which Britain, for one reason or another, has a comparative advantage.

Of course, the development would not in fact work in this way. There would be some lines in which British producers would be subject to recession. But the point is that the quantitatively important changes would lie not in the suppression of existing output, but in the better orientation of future expansion.

Nor should we be too much alarmed about those declines that will occur

Already we have to make our internal readjustments in the normal course of progress. In one year (1956) more than 100,000 persons were thrown out of work from certain consumer goods industries. It is true that about 50,000 lapsed from work altogether in this year, but these are more likely to have been those coming out of seasonal occupations than those displaced from the consumer trades; there was probably no great hardship owing to the heavy pull-in of unoccupied persons (some 600,000) in the preceding two years. Had the extrusion of 100,000 from certain industries occurred in 1954 or 1955, they would no doubt all have readily have found employment elsewhere. This is a far bigger switch than is ever likely to occur in one year in the course of the development of the common market. Provided that general policies for maintaining full employment are pursued, we need not expect any serious hardship for labour through the arrival of competitive goods from the continent.

But we need not deny that, if this project is put in train, many British firms ought to begin at once to think seriously about its long term implications. And many may not like the conclusions of their thinking. We speak of mass production. Having the United States in mind, we may ask how many main types of motor car should be produced in Europe. It is true that the population of the proposed common market is slightly greater than that of the United States, but, whatever benefits flow from the common market, it will be a very long time before its population can afford to buy so many cars per head. To say that there should be four different types of car—aside from specialities—is probably to admit a wholly uneconomic level of diversification. Yet this would mean that, at the most, Britain should not be producing more than one type of car. That is the kind of problem we are called upon to think about.

It is to be hoped that there will be greater co-ordination of monetary policy. There has been some similarity in the phasing of the trade cycle in the different countries of Europe in recent years, and not nearly as much mutual consultation about the modes of combating inflation or recession as that similarity should call for; the common market might be expected to engender a still greater similarity.

Co-ordination of policy by no means requires uniformity. Each country has to adapt its techniques to its own special problems, which will continue to remain different. The central problem in Britain in the recent phase of disinflation was how to finance the nationalised industries; this problem just did not arise in Germany. When in desperation Mr. Macmillan was driven to transfer the finance to the Exchequer from the system of independent issues by the Public Corporations, he was perfectly right to claim that this move would assist him in his policy of disinflation. The validity of that point depends on the very special features of the British money market. To any continental banker unversed in these mysteries, the move was bound to appear not disinflationary, but inflationary. I had the utmost difficulty in explaining to continental bankers that this really was not so. Any attempt to introduce uniformity of measures, such as, for instance, all countries raising the Bank Rate, or conducting open market operations (if they are able to), at the same time, would be disastrous, and render the last stage worse than the first. More intense mutual consultation and understanding are what is required.

There has been much talk of the possible need of flexible intra-European exchange rates, to secure balances of payments, in lieu of import restrictions when these are no longer available as corrective measures. The difficulty here is of course that the proper exchange rate cannot be determined by the intra-European balances alone. There is no reason why, in the true economic equilibrium, one European country should not have a chronic deficiency with the non-O.E.E.C. world, while some other member has a chronic surplus. The latter should then pay to the former a continuing stream of gold. Such a flow should not be taken as a sign of the need for any re-adjustment. The special features of the E.P.U. settlement have had some tendency to obscure this obvious point.

On the other hand the following point is also relevant and important. We might suppose—contrary unhappily to existing fact—that, prior to the opening of the common market, all the countries of Europe had exchange rates which were, roughly, correctly aligned in relation to the position of each *vis-à-vis* the whole of the rest of the world. Thus the exchange rate of each might be deemed to be in equilibrium; but the opening of the common market might alter this. It might well happen that at existing exchange rates some one country might have just outside the existing margin a plethora of goods, the flow of which is at present impeded by existing restrictions or tariffs, capable of under-cutting in other European markets; or some one country might be particularly vulnerable to competition by other European countries in goods just beyond the margin, *viz.* just kept out by the existing restrictions and tariffs. Thus an exchange rate which, given existing intra-European restrictions and tariffs, is an equilibrium one, might be revealed as wrong by the common market. This is a matter which will want looking at.

On the inception of E.P.U. generous lines of mutual automatic credits were set up. This seems to be something inherently desirable. More recently there has been a tendency to require larger gold payments, particularly owing to the very natural restiveness of chronic creditors, but also as part of the ideology of a return to convertibility. This strikes me as reactionary. Why should convertibility be regarded as precluding mutual credit? Indeed, the ardours of convertibility might make such mutual aid from time to time more desirable. I am sure it is preferable that the credit should be automatic, rather than vouchsafed *ad hoc* as the result of haggling and bargaining. The Federal Reserve System has provision for extending inter-district credits.

Some have held that the common market should have a common wage structure. No doubt this is a point on which vested interests will make much clamour, inveighing against low wages somewhere else. This appears to be a sphere in which economists should make a helpful contribution by expounding the doctrine of comparative costs. It is most unlikely that, for equilibrium, wages ought to be equal even in the major European countries. If existing differences are greater (or possibly less) than those required for equilibrium, this can be subsumed under the afore-mentioned problem of exchange rates.

The French press for an equalisation of social services also. They claim to have high standards. It is probable that the British standards are higher. It is claimed that a greater proportion of the finance required for the benefits in France falls upon industries as a cost of production. The British can make the counter claim that the part of their social services that is provided out of general taxation also falls on industry indirectly through the income tax or profits tax. The French counter-claim that there is a difference between payments, *e.g.* per person employed, that fall on costs, and those that only fall on profit, since, if profit is low, the firm in question gets relief from the payment, whereas the corresponding French firm does not. The quantitative importance of this may be exaggerated. There does not seem any reason in principle why the French point should not be conceded, although no doubt the bureaucracy would be up in arms, protesting the hideous administrative difficulties of making any change. One might even suggest to both parties that they should re-form their systems on the lines proposed by Lady Rhys Williams!

STOCKS AND QUANTITATIVE RESTRICTIONS

By J. R. SARGENT

For any country that participates in the proposed European Free Trade Area the gain that it reaps will be proportional to the disturbance it experiences. Economically the object of the enterprise is to rearrange the production of manufactures among the participants in order to take advantage of comparative costs, although it is also hoped—and certainly more frequently emphasised and taken for granted—that there will be absolute reductions in costs through the economies of scale to be realised from greater international specialisation. All this can hardly be gained without disturbance to the economies of the participants; indeed, the smaller the disturbances turn out to be, the more sceptical will one become of the economic importance of the enterprise. For the United Kingdom, however, its effects are not likely to be confined to a disturbance of the economy, in the sense that some industries will decline and others will expand. It is likely also to involve a deterioration of the terms of trade. This is not because the removal of our tariff on the manufactures of other participants creates a new demand for them and thus drives up their prices. The elasticity that there generally is in the supply of manufactures should moderate any such tendency; and to the extent that it does occur, we shall at the same time enjoy a rise in the prices of our exports as the tariffs of other participants also come tumbling down. The reason for expecting a deterioration of our terms of trade is rather the fear that we are a country whose tariff is high compared to that of other participants, so that when all tariffs have been removed, the temptation for us to buy more from the others will be greater than the temptation for them to buy more from us. It does not follow from this that our additional imports will exceed our additional exports, but there is at any rate a *prima facie* case for supposing so. If the supposition is correct, then we shall have to engineer a worsening of our terms of trade in order to regain equilibrium in the balance of payments. The hope is, of course, that the effect of worse terms of trade on real national income will be more than offset by the higher gross output that we achieve at home by concentrating our efforts on those industries at which we are most efficient.

How solid are the grounds for this hope, I shall not here discuss. Unless it is only shakily supported, we ought to grasp it without worrying overmuch about the disturbances we shall have to meet and the adjustments we shall have to make in our internal economy in the process. But the danger is that the Free Trade proposals will also denude our economy still further of defences against the sort of disturbance from which it emphatically ought to be protected. There are many pressures on the balance of payments which are temporary, and some of them may even be self-reversing. Examples of such pressures occur frequently in the history of the balance of payments of any predominantly primary producing country, resulting from varying harvests, or from speculative movements in demand such as that of 1950-1.

The balances of payments of predominantly manufacturing countries like the United Kingdom feel the backwash of these fluctuations. Another important source of temporary disturbance is mistakes of economic policy abroad, permitting there an outbreak of unintended inflation or deflation. In a world of imperfect knowledge we must expect the continual recurrence of such inroads on our balance of payments, even from the best-regulated economies. Moreover the United Kingdom makes its own particular contribution to the pathology of temporary fluctuations in the shape of the approximately biennial stock-cycle which has so aggravated our balance of payments difficulties. Now it is worse than pointless to allow a purely temporary pressure on the balance of payments to enforce the modification of important internal policies and the curtailment of domestic expenditure. There may be a case for laying the internal economy wide-open to the impact—to revive a somewhat outmoded concept—of a 'fundamental disequilibrium' and thus accelerating the adjustments that it must in any case make. But there is no case at all for laying it open to the impact of a temporary deficit. On the contrary, it should be insulated from it.

This is the reason, of course, why countries hold reserves of gold or foreign currency. The holding of such reserves is an expensive business, in that the money could be made to show a much higher yield to the country concerned if it were invested in some less liquid form; and this sacrifice is only made for the sake of the insulation which it gives to the internal economy from the impact of temporary pressures on its balance of payments. The degree of insulation which the United Kingdom can derive from the present level of its gold and dollar reserves is lamentably thin. But we do possess an additional insulator; we have our second-line reserve in the shape of stocks. When our balance of payments is threatened with a temporary deficit, we are not compelled to meet it from our monetary reserves; we may equally well meet it from our real reserves, by running down stocks or reducing the rate of stock-piling of imported goods or of other goods whose release will facilitate exports. There may be a case in general for holding our reserves against temporary pressures on our balance of payments in real rather than monetary form. There is certainly a case for ourselves in particular, now that our gold and dollar reserves afford us so little insulation, to design a better method of manipulating stocks in such a way as to offset these temporary pressures. The case is heavily reinforced by the fact that the present tendency of stock movements is, for reasons insufficiently known, actively to aggravate the pressures.

How, then, to manipulate stocks? It is often claimed that this can be done by a flexible monetary policy. We need not dismiss the claim. But the famous delicacy of Bank Rate as an instrument of policy is often such that its touch is hardly noticed. Certainly it had little effect in this direction in 1955, when again substantial stock-piling accompanied the balance of payments deficit. Let us simply say that it would be foolhardy to rely on monetary policy to manipulate the movement of stocks. Undoubtedly the most effective way to ensure the liquidation of stocks of imported goods in the face of a temporary deficit is to apply quantitative restrictions. The usual argument against employing quantitative restrictions against a balance of payments deficit is that they are inflationary in their effect on the internal economy. But this inflationary effect will not be felt in the first instance because manufacturers will draw from stock what they can no longer import. If the deficit continues for long enough, if it ceases to be temporary, these stocks will become exhausted; the inflationary effect of the quantitative restrictions will then no longer be absorbed and will call for some curtailment of internal expenditure. But against a temporary deficit they are an important weapon for defending internal expenditure from the impact of irrelevant external fluctuations. They will enforce more effectively than monetary policy can be relied upon to do the liquidation of the country's real reserves against temporary deficits, in circumstances where further liquidation of its monetary reserves is impossible.

There is every reason to expect that when the European Free Trade Area is being negotiated, there will be strong pressure to limit the power of members to use quantitative restrictions even more stringently than it is now limited by the Liberalisation Code of O.E.E.C.[1] It is obviously a good thing, assuming that there are long-term gains to be had from the scheme, that quantitative restrictions should, no more than any of the other distorting factors which it aims to abolish, be allowed to interfere with the long-term readjustment of the economy in the direction of comparative advantage. Hence the final agreement on the scheme should *limit the permissible duration* of quantitative restrictions once they have been imposed; but it should *not limit the power to impose them for periods of time within this duration* in circumstances when it would be unwise for the country concerned to meet a temporary deficit by running down its monetary reserves. It is good that for the sake of an all-round improvement of productive efficiency we should consent to the eventual abolition of quantitative restrictions of a permanent or semi-permanent type; but to agree to abandon their temporary use would be folly. It is, of course, a folly which the present government is already committing; but if they allowed it to be written into an international treaty, it would be far harder to revoke.

The abandonment of the power to make temporary use of quantitative restrictions should be contemplated only if the internal economy can be found some other means of insulation from the impact of temporary fluctuations in the balance of payments. Are there any such? One would be a softening of E.P.U., designed to reduce the claim on the gold reserves of a deficit of any given size. This would involve reversing the recent powerfully-supported trend to harden E.P.U. settlements. It also raises the question whether a soft E.P.U. would be used for settlements, when sterling can be

---

[1] The recent change of Chancellor makes it less likely that the pressure will be resisted. Mr. Macmillan has shown signs of being less dogmatic in his dislike of controls than Mr. Thorneycroft, and certainly less dogmatic than most of those whose advice a Conservative Chancellor would be inclined to take.

sold in New York and Zurich at a rate which the Exchange Equalisation Account will support if necessary. This would not be an insuperable objection. For the E.E.A. has it within its power to discourage the sale of sterling in these markets by supporting the sterling rate in a very jumpy way and, while keeping its average level at the height desired, making its level at any particular moment extremely uncertain. One hopes that in any case it does this rather than give the rate a dead-pan stability. This is quite different from the argument for a floating rate; it is merely a method which might be used to encourage settlements, at a fixed rate, through a soft E.P.U. despite the possibility of converting sterling more fully elsewhere than in E.P.U. Possibly a floating rate would act as an insulator against temporary balance of payments fluctuations by encouraging capital flows in the requisite sense; but it is difficult to have much confidence in this.

Instead of seeking insulation by measures to protect our monetary reserves, can we find it by manipulating stocks—our real reserves—by methods other than quantitative restrictions? If stocks are sensitive to the short-term rate of interest, then in the face of a temporary deficit we might attempt to decumulate them by a severe stiffening of this rate. But at the same time we should have to prevent any consequent rise in the long-term rate, since this would disturb internal long-term investment and we should have failed to insulate the internal economy as we intended. A rise in the short rate combined with stability in the long could be achieved by accompanying conventional measures of credit contraction by a deliberate process of unfunding, whereby the government would increase its short-term borrowing in order to buy its own long-term securities.[1] While conventional open-market operations were levering up interest rates generally, this short-term borrowing would give a further lift to the short rate and the application of the proceeds to the purchase of long-term securities would drive the long rate back towards its original level. The danger that this would tend to increase the secondary liquidity ratio of the commercial banks,[2] and thus encourage an expansion of advances which might neutralise the effort to enforce a reduction of stocks, could be met by the use of Treasury Deposit Receipts to mop up any surplus liquidity that there may be. The major disadvantage of this effort to enforce a very high short rate divorced from the long rate is the high cost to the balance of payments, since a substantial proportion of the short-term debt is externally held. An alternative approach to the aim we have in mind, and one which does not share this disadvantage, is the tax on bank advances suggested by Professor Hicks in a previous Bulletin symposium. But this will not only disturb such long-term investments as depend upon bank advances for their finance, of which there may be a number in their early stages; it will also have an effect on the long-term rate of interest by

---

[1] Without credit creation, that is. The government is inclined to turn to creating credit, when it wants to sell more Treasury Bills.

[2] If the short-term securities sold by the government were all bought by the public and not by the banks, and the long-term securities bought by the government were all sold by the public and not by the banks, the banks' liquidity ratio would be unaffected

tempting short-term borrowers to turn from the banks to the long-term capital market.

None of these possibilities seems to offer startling promise as an insulator against temporary fluctuations in the balance of payments. There is one, however, which is ready to hand and of which more might be made. The government itself is quite a considerable holder of stocks. At the end of 1955 these stood at about £450 million, having declined by £230 million in the two preceding years owing to the decline in the area of state trading. Nevertheless £450 million is enough to enable the government to give the internal economy some degree of insulation by skilfully phasing variations in the figure. It is true that £260 million of the total consisted of strategic stocks; but the freedom with which these can be run up and down for purely economic reasons should not be thought of as non-existent. In recent years government stocks have tended to share the perversity of private stocks; changes in them have helped to aggravate rather than offset pressure on the balance of payments, especially in 1951.[1] The government could make a greater effort to co-ordinate the stock-piling activities of its various departments and agencies, and to direct them for the purpose of absorbing pressures of a temporary nature.

Perhaps, then, there is something that can be done to improve the insulation of the economy, now that the normal equipment for this, the gold and dollar reserves, has worn so thin—and now that the strain upon it had been steadily increasing with the drift to convertibility. But it hardly seems to add up to an amount which could justify us in giving up our right to resort to the temporary use of quantitative restrictions. We should submit readily to having clauses in the final treaty which limit the length of time for which restrictions imposed against temporary deficits can be maintained; for if there are gains to be had from free trade in the long run, we should allow our economy to be open to the influence of comparative costs and to the long-run changes in its structure which will be the price of those gains. But we must retain the power to protect our internal economy—and in particular our investment programme—from being disturbed by irrelevant temporary fluctuations of the balance of payments; and this means that we cannot throw onto the scrap-heap the weapon of quantitative restrictions.

[1] The relative movements of government and private stocks in 1954–5 are difficult to disentangle because of the steady change-over from government to private trading.

A POSITIVE CONTRIBUTION?

By R. F. KAHN

I see no reason for questioning the view, which seems to be fairly generally accepted, that if *in any case* there is going to be a European Customs Union, comprising the six Schumann plan countries, it is better for this country that we should join the projected free trade area rather than that we should stay out—at any rate if we can confine our participation to non-agricultural products. The interesting question is not that one but whether, from the point of view of this country, we should welcome and encourage the scheme as a development which is likely to work out positively in our own economic interests or whether it is really most unfortunate and awkward that the issue has arisen at all.

One reason why there has been so little opposition in this country to participation in the scheme is that most of those who dislike it feel that more harm would result from staying out than from coming in. It is not merely of academic interest to enquire whether this pessimistic attitude is justified. For its justification turns on issues of policy in the administration of a free trade area; and it is related to the question whether or not it is in the interests of this country to work constructively for the adoption of the scheme—or at least it would be so related but for the unpalatable fact that the scheme would offer greater advantages to some of the participants if we did not take part ourselves (so that if we threaten to stay out our bluff is only too likely to be called).

The pessimistic attitude has *prima facie* much to recommend it. If I do not adopt it unhesitatingly, it is because I am myself pessimistic about the alternatives to closer western European integration. If there were reason to think that something might still be made of the Commonwealth and the sterling area, a closer affiliation with Europe, even though unavoidable, might be regretted on account of consequent losses elsewhere. But the tide has turned strongly against closer affiliation with Commonwealth and sterling area countries. The drift against discriminatory import control in the sterling area will, it is true, be encouraged by the mere fact of a closer linking of this country with Europe. But there is no evidence—quite the contrary—that even in the absence of such closer linking with Europe anything effective would be done to maintain a fruitful relationship with other parts of the world. Indeed, over the next few years economic statesmanship is likely to be heavily strained over the completely negative task of curbing the rate of utilisation of the sterling balances owned inside the sterling area.

In the second place, I am not completely pessimistic about the way in which a closely-knit western Europe might be administered. Hostages will not be, it may be expected as well as hoped, altogether lightly handed over to fortune. Free trade is not such a very popular idea, and some of the reasons for this are good reasons. If free trade is to be the aim, even though in a limited sphere, the sceptics have a golden opportunity for insisting on safeguards. One great advantage that Europe offers over either the Commonwealth or the sterling area for the exercise of a harmonising influence on the pattern of trade is the existence of central organs of co-ordination. The O.E.E.C. already exists and the Customs Union will rely on a new European Commission. It is true that the prospect of a two-tier system of administration is not in itself inviting. But it has to be accepted that the Customs Union is likely to be run on rather different principles from the wider free trade area. Within the common market of the Customs Union it is laid down that, except during the transitional period, restrictions on trade are to be reimposed in the event of balance of payments difficulties only in default of the granting of the necessary credits, on which reliance is placed as a means of avoiding restrictions on trade. On the other hand, in the discussions about a looser association by this country, and probably others, in the form of a free trade area, there has been considerable emphasis on import control as a temporary alleviation for a country in balance of payments difficulties. If this emphasis is to be justified by the outcome, the O.E.E.C.—or such *ad hoc* body as may be set up for the purpose—will have to play a more positive role than it has for some years. An enormous amount depends on the manner in which the rules are worked out.

My optimism, it must be admitted, is precariously poised. It has to be recognised that on the whole those who supply the positive impetus towards the free trade area—those who really believe in it as opposed to sceptics who regard it as an inescapable but sad necessity—are those who hanker after the free operation of economic forces and are unable to see the need or feasibility of tempering influences. Unless the sceptics exert a marked influence, in the various countries concerned, over the negotiation of the rules, my optimism will prove unjustified. At the moment optimism is in some measure kept alive by various public statements, which seem to suggest that in the years to come import control may play a more important part than it has in the last two years in softening the influence on internal policy of short-period fluctuations in the balance of payments. For example, Mr. Harold Macmillan, then Chancellor of the Exchequer, referring to import quotas : ' Those, too, would be progressively abolished between the members of the free trade area subject to a strict proviso that they might be restored temporarily at any time by a country faced with balance of payments difficulties '.[1]

Another benefit to be looked for from closer economic collaboration in western Europe is greater readiness to alter exchange rates and more flexible arrangements for securing alterations. Here again one has to admit a serious danger. The word ' harmonization ' is exercising a baneful effect—largely under French influence—on those concerned with working out the basis for the Customs Union. It is illustrated by the claim that it is necessary to standardise the length of the working week and to eliminate exceptions to the principle of equal pay for equal work before free trade can be entertained. Such ideas are alien to the principles of free trade and it is reasonable to hope

[1] House of Commons, November 26th, 1956, *Official Report*, col. 40.

that their stupidity will gradually be recognised. But at the same time greater recognition is needed of the incompatibility of free trade with the present-day sanctity of exchange rates, which is almost worthy of the gold standard.

This sanctity is partly attributable to the view that some magic attaches to the existence of obstacles to trade which enables a country maintaining them to allow its money costs and prices to follow an independent course and which can therefore preserve a policy of full employment irrespective of what is happening elsewhere. But this idea is valid only in relation to fluctuations and not to trends. If a country's full employment policy results in a secular rise of its money costs above those of its competitors, obstacles to trade will prevent the development of a growing adverse balance of payments only if they are progressively increasing in height. That is clearly unthinkable. It is a different matter if one is contemplating fluctuations rather than persistent trends. Then this point of view has much force, and it must be recognised that partial elimination of tariffs and import restrictions will render a country more vulnerable to fluctuations in its trading position. These fluctuations may operate over longer periods than can be properly dealt with by temporary import control and advances of credits. This is why a change of attitude towards alterations of exchange rates seems essential. If this change takes place it is likely to mean that more has been gained than has been lost by way of restraining the influence on domestic policy of external factors.

It is not, of course, sufficient that adequate provision be made for the necessary adjustments, both temporary and permanent. They are necessary to render merely tolerable the idea of the free trade area. But if it is to be positively attractive one has to enquire into the advantages of free trade and to secure a favourable response to the enquiry. It is here principally that I differ both from the advocates and from the critics. I tend to agree with the latter, though I go less far than some of them, that, in the European context, it is easy to exaggerate the importance of the economies of division of labour and of specialisation, of the spur to efficiency provided by extra competition and of the erosion of profit margins. Much of this will come about anyway. And for the rest, trial by ordeal, which is what free trade will mean if business men allow it to operate seriously, is a poor and brutal way of deciding how the principle of comparative costs is ultimately to operate (even though there is to be a transition period of twelve or fifteen years). As between one branch of manufacture and another, there is usually little in it, apart from historical accident; and international agreement designed to secure specialisation, backed by control over new investment and import control, even if its basis was necessarily somewhat arbitrary, would be speedier and less destructive in achieving the objective of free trade. It is of course possible that the idea of control over large expansion projects, operated from the centre, will in the course of time be extended from the Coal and

Steel Community to the Customs Union and the free trade area generally, the European Commission and the O.E.E.C. constituting the necessary machinery.

If the proposals were designed to apply the principle of comparative costs as between industry and agriculture it would again be a very different matter. In the Customs Union, but not generally in the free trade area, agriculture is to be included in the common market, and it is recognised, in the case of the Customs Union, that agriculture is one of the sectors in which the most significant results could be expected from liberalisation. However, it is hard to conceive at least for some of the countries concerned that alternative methods of supporting the farmer will not be continued, and indeed developed.

All this may be true. But a free trade area is not the same as a free trade world. Precisely because it does not comprise the whole world the gain to its members is not confined to the economies in the use of resources which are associated with free trade and to the improvements to efficiency in which free trade may result. There is the ' trade-diverting ' effect to be considered as well as the ' trade-creating ' effect.[1] Quite apart from anything else, the formation of a free trade area means an improvement—compared with what would otherwise, at the same point of time (we are of course looking ten years and more ahead!), be the situation—in the balance of payments position of the area, and therefore of most, it not of all, its members. Unless this country turns out to be especially vulnerable to European competition in its domestic market, it can hope to enjoy a reasonable share of that improvement. Placed as it is, and as it is likely to continue to be placed, that is a very acceptable benefit. It is partly the result of the participants in the free trade area being readier to buy from one another, as against the outside world, so that for most of them, if not for all, the demand for exports is raised by more than the demand for imports. This is additional to any improvement in the balance of payments position resulting from achievement of the real economies of free trade.

The development of a greater actual export surplus by the free trade area will be in conflict with the opportunities for investment inside the area, rendered more attractive both by the widening of the market and—certainly in the Customs Union, possibly in the rest of the free trade area—by greater mobility of funds between European countries. On the whole it seems probable that the improvement in the balance of payments position will be taken out in a higher level of money wages relatively to money wage levels outside the area rather than in a greater surplus on income account. This will come about partly because deflationary action against the upward pressure

---

[1] J. Viner, *The Customs Union Issue*. It is, I think, convenient to retain Professor Viner's phrases, and in a broad way the distinction which underlies them, despite the penetrating examination of his analysis at the hands of Professor James Meade (*The Theory of Customs Unions*: see also *Trade and Welfare*, chapter XXXII).

of money wages will be less necessary, partly because devalution will be less necessary than would otherwise be the case.

In so far as the pure diversion effect of free trade in the area preponderates over the real economies of free trade, the balancing of trade will require a movement of the terms of trade adverse to the outside world. And in so far as it is *only* the diversion effect which operates, the benefit to the members of the free trade area is achieved at the expense of other countries.

The possibility of such adverse effects on other countries is a very real one. It is obviously much in the minds of the Canadians, who were looking forward to a rapid growth of their exports of manufactured goods. It may be particularly serious for a country like Malta (if not "integrated") or Israel, which needs a large expansion of exports of miscellaneous manufactured goods in order to achieve a bare equilibrium.

It is of course possible that the adjustment of the pattern of trade will be partly achieved by a lowering of obstacles against imports from outside countries, and so not entirely by the attainment of a higher relative level of money wages. In any case it is probable that there will be less resort to quantitative import control than would otherwise be called for, but this does not necessarily mean a larger volume of imports of the goods affected. In so far as it is the diversion effect which preponderates, some relaxation of import control will be compatible with a lower volume of imports. It is only if the lowering of obstacles is taken beyond a certain point that it will positively contribute to an increase of imports. And this will be possible only for particular commodities, not for imports as a whole, except in so far as Europe's exporting powers are positively improved as a result of real economies of free trade.

The indications thus hinted at of the effects on under-developed countries are not particularly encouraging. Adverse effects on the terms on which they exchange their products for manufactured goods from Europe are only too compatible with benefit to the European countries themselves. There remains, however, the question of the extent to which the improvement in the European balance of payments position is likely to be taken out in additional financing by European countries of under-developed countries. Even if a large favourable balance of payments on income account is maintained after European monetary reserves have been adequately built up, there is the absorption by the organised security markets of the United States, and more particularly of Canada, to be reckoned with, and possibly a strong move towards export of capital for political reasons. The application of a favourable balance to the development of backward areas will turn on the readiness of Governments to intervene as financing agencies and to retain exchange control. The main point, however, is the competition, already mentioned, with investment inside Europe, which makes it unlikely that, except perhaps for a few years, the creation of the free trade area will result in the maintenance of a really substantial surplus on the balance of payments. But the reasons for this are not at all unfavourable if looked at from a narrow European standpoint.

CONCLUSION

By G. D. N. Worswick

It was never the hope of the editor that all the answers to the Customs Union and Free Trade Area proposals would be provided in a Symposium prepared as quickly as this, but it was hoped that all the important questions might be raised. No particular aspect of the proposals was suggested as a topic to the individual contributors. They were sent a draft of Mr. Black's introductory account of the statistical background and invited to write about whatever they liked. Thanks would in any case be due for the interest aroused by each individual author, but an editor's gratitude is redoubled in that he is not left with any feeling that there are important omissions which he himself must do something to repair. The authors have chosen to write at diverse levels, about different aspects and from different points of view; between them they touch on, and often make proposals about, all the issues that seem likely to arise. Not that the complementarity of subject necessarily denotes agreement. Where the authors do overlap there is sometimes sharp divergence. Professor Kahn, for example, has little patience with the idea of ' harmonisation ' of social services, while Mr. Harrod expresses implicit approval in his final sentence, though one suspects that he may have been guided here as much by considerations of political tactics as of ecomonic principle.

I shall not attempt any synthesis, nor any systematic listing of points of agreement and disagreement. Rather I should like to pick up two or three threads which seem to me especially important. First is the question of the long-term gains to be expected from a Free Trade Area. Opinions here are widely divergent. Contrast, for example, what Mr. Harrod has to say about the motor car market with Professor Johnson's argument that ' the likelihood of economies of scale as such is extremely small '. Professor Johnson's observation that there are potential economies of scale *within* national markets which have not been exploited is highly relevant: but the removal of tariffs must surely have *some* effect in assisting mass production.

Professor Johnson takes Mr. Black to task for implicitly accepting the popular terms of the debate too readily, and despite a plethora of statistics, for not providing much of the material required. He sets out the economic criteria which should be applied and adds: ' a corresponding quantitative exercise is called for, but will not be provided here '. Is this not a trifle disingenuous? Later on Professor Johnson observes that ' a calculation of the potential net benefit from participation in the Free Trade area would obviously require a great deal of information on existing tariff levels, demand functions and production possibilities in Britain and elsewhere '. This is a tall order. To take the apparently simplest point first: as Mr. Black points out, the mere summarisation of existing tariff levels is not possible for any independent researcher. Trade figures are not broken down in such detail as to correspond to each separate tariff item: within any 'group' of export or import items several different tariff rates may operate. As for demand functions and production possibilities, econometric methods are certainly not able to churn out elasticities of demand and supply (if such oldfashioned terms may be permitted). This is not to say that no factual light can be thrown on the ' potential net benefit '. A quantitative exercise could profitably be undertaken, not by any individual or research institute, but by the respective governments. The kinds of questions which need to be put are of course formally those set out by Professor Johnson: but they need to be put in the context of detailed practical experience in each individual trade, and only the Board of Trade (and its opposite numbers elsewhere) is in a position to call upon the experience required. No doubt some enquiries along these lines have already been made. It would be most valuable if they could be generalised to cover at least the major trades likely to be affected and the results of the enquiry published in a form which makes clear the assumptions upon which the questions were put. For it is in the actual examination of, and comment upon, the assumptions that professional economists might reasonably be expected to make some useful contribution.

It is argued by several contributors that the full working out of the Free Trade area may give rise to structural balance of payments problems which will need to be allowed for by adjustment of price levels or exchange rates. A quantitative exercise should at least throw light on the direction of the changes needed, if not providing precise answers to the amounts of the changes.

It is natural, and often fatal, for an economist to analyse a problem of this kind in two parts—the long-term, or structural, adjustment and short-term fluctuations. I should like to comment on Mr. Sargent's interesting suggestion, but before doing so, I must take up the problem of Germany. At the end of the Second War, Mr. Balogh was one of the most ardent protagonists of the ' regional bloc ', a stick with which he vigorously beat the advocates of I.M.F., I.T.O. and other manifestations of non-discriminatory multilateralism. Is his present attitude just sour grapes?

There has been more than one attempt in history to unify the European economy. Hitler had the idea in his New Order. In that conception the economic basis of military power would have been kept within Germany itself: the satellite countries would have had their heavy industrial capacity strictly limited, and their economies confined to agriculture and light industries. The hegemony of Germany would have been perpetuated through a monopoly of the economic resources for war. Such a system was repulsive—but it might well have worked.

If I understand him aright, the danger that Mr. Balogh fears is not the economic subjection of Europe by deliberate and malicious use of military power but by the misguided application of a potentially beneficent economic idea. If we, and other European countries, abrogate both tariffs and quantitative restrictions, might not a persistently creditor Germany, whose productivity was rising faster than elsewhere, ultimately drive the other members into deflation and stagnation? After all, such things have happened before. Of course, if we invoke the role of U.S.A. in the world-wide depression of the early nineteen-thirties, we are told that things have changed, and that we are all Keynesians now. That may or may not be true in America, but Mr. Harrod's experience with continental bankers seems to suggest that they at any rate have not yet seen the Keynesian light.[1] And is it altogether fanciful to see in the anxiety of the French to get Germany to pay for North Africa now, as the price of French co-operation in the Customs Union, a calculation that France may be little strengthened, and even permanently weakened, by the Customs Union?

Whether or not these fears are exaggerated, it is surely right to put great emphasis upon the instruments for the channelling of funds for developing the economies of all the member countries. Even if it be true that thinking in matters of domestic economic policy has been revolutionised by Keynes, our thinking in terms of international instruments of expansion still lags painfully behind.[2]

Several contributors make the point that the British Government's insistence on the restoration of quantitative restrictions as the basic safeguard against violent *short-term* fluctuations in the balance of payments is not consistent with the long-term aims of the proposals. No doubt no British Government can bind itself to refrain from using *any* policy instrument in such a way that it would be helpless to counter large-scale unemployment. Nevertheless, Mr. Harrod is surely right that generous automatic credits are inherently desirable. Mr. Sargent's proposals, too, concerning the use of stocks as a parallel ' reserve ' are worth further study.

On February 12th the Ministers met at O.E.E.C. to consider the report of a Working Party on various aspects of the parallel Customs Union and Free Trade area proposals. Already initial positions have been taken up, and the sharp divergence between Denmark and Britain over the exclusion of agricultural products has become apparent. That negotiations will be protracted and difficult is more than likely, because the two sets of proposals do raise a number of strictly technical questions of great complexity. The danger that the absorption of economic brain power in technical detail may obscure judgement of the ultimate consequences is only too likely to be re-inforced by the political desire in this kind of situation to reach agreement for agreement's sake.

Professor Kahn is pessimistic about reviving interest in a more positive approach to the economic development of the Commonwealth. His pessimism

[1] Mr. Harrod will, I trust, forgive me for quoting him out of context. But it is not unreasonable to suggest that a banker who jibs at a strictly disinflationary manoeuvre *via* the public accounts would object twice over if the purpose was to expand the economy.

[2] The idea of establishing a link between long-term lending and chronic balance of payments deficits was fully worked out in 1943 by Kalecki, Schumacher and Balogh (*cf.* ' New Plans for International Trade ', supplement to the Bulletin of the Institute of Statistics, 1943). The notion was officially picked up in the report of the United Nations Experts on ' National and International Measures for Full Employment ' in 1949. Unfortunately however, these ideas have never been incorporated in any of the post-war international or inter-regional arrangements.

will certainly not be reduced by the current suggestion that the British Government's reference to the Commonwealth as the justification for excluding agricultural products is merely a cloak to cover up the protection of British agriculture. One can only express the hope that he is too pessimistic and that all attempts to make closer relations with the Commonwealth have not been officially abandoned. It is certain, however, that we shall not withdraw from the European negotiations and here there are two ultimate consequences which should never be lost sight of.

Firstly, Britain as a one time Imperial Power must surely lay great emphasis on the need to narrow the great disparities of income and wealth between the low and high income areas of Europe itself. A scheme which led to the perpetuation of the depressed areas of France and Southern Italy would not be an appealing one. Secondly, while protection in its various forms can mitigate the impact of external changes on Britain itself, it remains true that our own future depends very much on securing a higher rate of investment than we have been able to achieve so far in the post-war years. We should not, therefore, support proposals which would make this objective even more difficult.

THE FREE TRADE PROPOSALS

Part II

A Further Appraisal

EUROPE'S TRADE AND ECONOMIC PROGRESS IN THE 1950s

By J. BLACK

The object of this note is to provide, first, an up-to-date cross-section of the geographical distribution and commodity composition of British and European trade; and, second, a brief survey of the trends in production, trade, prices and exchange reserves in Britain and certain European countries over the past five years. These are intended to provide a basis for an assessment of the prospects of continued growth in the economies of Western Europe, and for a discussion of the desirability of the alternatives for Britain of increasing integration with the other European economies *via* entry to the Common Market or association with it on terms acceptable to the other members, or increasing exclusion from it *via* the gradual rise of discrimination by tariffs and quotas against the exports of non-members.

I. THE DIRECTION OF EUROPEAN TRADE IN 1957

Exports. Table 1 shows the destinations of exports in 1957, at current prices in U.S. $mn., of Britain, of the Common Market countries, i.e. W. Germany, France, Italy, Belgium and Luxemburg, and the Netherlands; and of four other countries, Denmark, Norway, Sweden and Austria, which are at present seeking an acceptable form of association with the Common Market. Table 2 shows the derived percentage distribution of each country's exports to the various destinations. The geographical distribution of Britain's exports in 1957 was significantly different from that of the rest of Western Europe. The rest of the Sterling Area and the U.S.A. and Canada were the destination of larger proportions of British exports than of those of any other country shown in Table 2.

The Sterling Area took 45 per cent of Britain's exports; the proportion of the other countries' exports going to the rest of the Streling Area (i.e. excluding Britain) varied from 4 per cent of Danish to 9½ per cent of West German exports, the West European average being 7½ per cent.

The U.S.A. and Canada took 13½ per cent of British exports, compared with percentages for other countries ranging from 4½ per cent of Austrian to 10 per cent of Italian exports, the European average being 7½ per cent. The proportion of European exports going to Britain varied from 2½ per cent of Austrian to 28 per cent of Danish exports; but while the Common Market countries averaged 5½ per cent, 17½ per cent of the exports of the other four went to Britain.

All the other destinations shown accounted for larger proportions of European than of British exports. Continental Western Europe as a whole

B

TABLE 1. *Exports in 1957 by Destination U.S. $mn.*

	World	U.S.A. and Canada	Britain	Rest of Sterling Area	Continental W. Europe	Common Market	Other Four[1]	Rest of W. Europe	Other	Territories etc.[2]	Asia[3]	U.S.S.R.[4]	Latin America[5]
Britain ...	9,310	1,235	—	4,201	2,322	1,288	789	245	1,552	381	468	194	461
W. Germany ...	8,575	695	335	806	4,666	2,503	1,392	771	2,073	391	582	285	699
France ...	5,067	278	278	223	1,824	1,277	205	342	2,464	1,820	247	140	213
Italy ...	2,540	259	158	233	1,156	635	193	328	734	194	161	114	231
Belgium & Lux. ...	3,186	309	178	209	1,832	1,468	216	148	658	237	125	88	179
Netherlands ...	3,098	180	337	246	1,728	1,289	321	118	607	178	181	66	125
Common Market	22,466	1,721	1,286	1,717	11,206	7,172	2,327	1,707	6,536	2,820	1,296	693	1,447
Denmark ...	1,156	105	323	48	523	349	150	24	157	38	26	35	55
Norway ...	820	59	164	62	386	231	134	21	149	27	20	43	55
Sweden ...	2,137	117	383	123	1,102	704	336	62	412	85	50	106	158
Austria ...	978	42	24	55	589	483	31	75	268	50	39	143	36
Other Four ...	5,091	323	894	288	2,600	1,767	651	182	986	200	135	327	304
Common Market + Other Four	27,557	2,044	2,180	2,005	13,806	8,939	2,978	1,889	7,522	3,020	1,431	1,020	1,751

[1] Denmark, Norway, Sweden and Austria.
[2] Territories of Continental Western Europe, *plus* Morocco, Tunisia, Finland, Spain and Yugoslavia.
[3] Non-Sterling Middle Eastern and other Far Eastern Countries.
[4] U.S.S.R., Other Eastern European Countries and China.
[5] Dollar-plus-Non-Dollar Countries.
Source: U.N. Commodity Trace Statistics, Series D. Vol. VII, No. 4.

TABLE 2. *Exports in 1957 by Destination. Per cent.*

	World	U.S.A. and Canada	Britain	Rest of Sterling Area	Continental W. Europe	Common Market	Other Four[1]	Rest of W. Europe	Other	Territories etc.[2]	Asia[3]	U.S.S.R.[4]	Latin America[5]
Britain	100	13.3	—	45.1	25.0	13.8	8.5	2.6	16.7	4.1	5.0	2.1	5.0
W. Germany ...	100	8.1	3.9	9.4	54.5	29.2	16.2	9.0	24.2	4.6	6.8	3.3	8.2
France	100	5.5	5.5	4.4	36.0	25.2	4.0	6.7	48.6	35.9	4.9	2.8	4.2
Italy	100	10.2	6.2	9.2	45.5	25.0	7.6	12.9	28.9	7.6	6.3	4.5	9.1
Belgium & Lux. ...	100	9.7	5.6	6.6	57.5	46.0	6.8	4.6	20.6	7.4	3.9	2.8	5.6
Netherlands ...	100	5.8	10.9	7.9	55.8	41.6	10.4	3.8	19.6	5.7	5.8	2.1	4.0
Common Market	100	7.7	5.7	7.6	49.9	31.9	10.4	7.6	29.0	12.5	5.8	3.1	6.4
Denmark ...	100	9.1	28.0	4.2	45.2	30.2	13.0	2.1	13.6	3.3	2.3	3.0	4.8
Norway ...	100	7.2	20.0	7.6	47.1	28.2	16.3	2.6	18.2	3.3	2.4	5.2	6.7
Sweden ...	100	5.5	17.9	5.8	51.6	33.0	15.7	2.9	19.3	4.0	2.3	5.0	7.4
Austria ...	100	4.3	2.5	5.6	60.2	49.4	3.2	7.7	27.4	5.1	4.0	14.6	3.7
Other Four ...	100	6.3	17.6	5.7	51.1	34.7	12.8	3.6	19.4	3.9	2.7	6.4	6.0
Common Market + Other Four	100	7.4	7.9	7.3	50.2	32.4	10.8	6.9	27.3	11.0	5.2	3.7	6.4

[1] Denmark, Norway, Sweden and Austria.
[2] Territories of Continental Western Europe, *plus* Morocco, Tunisia, Finland, Spain and Yugoslavia.
[3] Non-Sterling Middle Eastern and other Far Eastern Countries.
[4] U.S.S.R., Other Eastern European Countries and China.
[5] Dollar-plus-Non-Dollar Countries.
Source: U.N. Commodity Trace Statistics, Series D. Vol. VII, No. 4.

took 25 per cent of British exports, but proportions of the exports of European countries varying from 36 per cent for France to 60 per cent for Austria, with a European average of 50 per cent.

The differences between the proportions of British and European exports going to the ' other four ', Denmark, Norway, Sweden and Austria, were much less marked than the differences in the proportions going to either the Common Market countries or the rest of Western Europe. The Common Market countries took 14 per cent of British exports, but proportions of each others' exports varying from 25 per cent for Italy to 46 per cent for Belgium, with an average of 32 per cent; the Common Market countries also bought $34\frac{1}{2}$ per cent of the exports of the ' other four '. The other four countries took $8\frac{1}{2}$ per cent of British exports, $10\frac{1}{2}$ per cent of the Common Market countries' exports, and 13 per cent of each others'. The rest of Western Europe took $2\frac{1}{2}$ per cent of British exports, $7\frac{1}{2}$ per cent of the Common Market countries', and $3\frac{1}{2}$ per cent of the four countries' exports.

The proportion of British exports going to all other destinations, i.e. everywhere except the U.S.A. and Canada, the Sterling Area, and Continental Western Europe, was $16\frac{1}{2}$ per cent. The proportions of European exports going to these destinations varied from $13\frac{1}{2}$ per cent of Danish to $48\frac{1}{2}$ per cent of French exports. 29 per cent of the total Common Market countries' exports went to these destinations, and $19\frac{1}{2}$ per cent of those of the ' other four '.

Similar differences show up for each of the four divisions into which ' other destinations ' have been divided. The territories of Continental Western Europe, plus an assorted group—Morocco, Tunisia, Spain, Finland and Yugoslavia—of countries in or near Europe, accounted for 4 per cent of British exports. The proportions of the exports of European countries other than France going to these destinations varied from $3\frac{1}{2}$ per cent for Denmark and Norway to $7\frac{1}{2}$ per cent for Italy; but as 36 per cent of French exports went to these areas—mainly to present or former French territories—the average for West Europe as a whole was raised to 11 per cent.

The non-sterling parts of the Middle and Far East took 5 per cent of British exports, 6 per cent of Common Market and $2\frac{1}{2}$ per cent of the other four countries' exports. The U.S.S.R., Eastern Europe and China took 2 per cent of British, 3 per cent of the Common Market countries', and $6\frac{1}{2}$ per cent of the other four countries' exports. Latin America took 5 per cent of British, and $6\frac{1}{2}$ per cent of European exports.

Imports. Table 3 shows British and European imports classified by country of origin, in U.S. $mn; and Table 4 shows the derived percentage distribution. The differences between Britain and Europe are similar to those for exports.

The rest of the Sterling Area supplied 38 per cent of British imports,

TABLE 3. *Imports in 1957 by Origin U.S. $mn.*

	World	U.S.A. and Canada	Britain	Rest of Sterling Area	Continental W. Europe	Common Market	Other Four[1]	Rest of W. Europe	Other	Territories etc.[2]	Asia[3]	U.S.S.R.[4]	Latin America[5]
Britain ...	11,412	2,256	—	4,320	2,549	1,375	965	209	2,287	595	331	347	968
W. Germany ...	7,499	1,532	266	758	3,010	1,763	893	354	1,933	458	371	273	802
France ...	6,112	887	227	999	1,693	1,305	214	174	2,306	1,569	300	148	284
Italy ...	3,625	742	179	567	1,260	784	308	168	877	191	326	115	243
Belgium & Lux. ...	3,432	467	282	283	1,748	1,495	167	86	652	280	142	69	148
Netherlands ...	4,105	593	330	275	1,999	1,689	228	82	908	151	314	87	345
Common Market	24,773	4,221	1,284	2,882	9,710	7,036	1,810	864	6,676	2,649	1,453	692	1,822
Denmark ...	1,353	137	331	10	697	491	177	29	178	34	33	49	62
Norway ...	1,274	170	222	39	673	398	252	23	170	37	35	48	48
Sweden ...	2,428	325	336	118	1,224	956	206	62	425	84	82	84	176
Austria ...	1,128	150	47	41	687	585	27	75	203	39	19	117	27
Other Four ...	6,183	782	936	208	3,281	2,430	662	189	976	194	169	298	313
Common Market + Other Four	30,956	5,003	2,220	3,090	12,991	9,446	2,472	1,053	7,652	2,843	1,622	990	2,135

[1] Denmark, Norway, Sweden and Austria.
[2] Territories of Continental Western Europe, *plus* Morocco, Tunisia, Finland, Spain and Yugoslavia.
[3] Non-Sterling Middle Eastern and other Far Eastern Countries.
[4] U.S.S.R., Other Eastern European Countries and China.
[5] Dollar-plus-Non-Dollar Countries.
Source: U.N. Commodity Trace Statistics, Series D. Vol. VII, No. 4.

TABLE 4. *Imports in 1957 by Origin. Per cent.*

	World	U.S.A. and Canada	Britain	Rest of Sterling Area	Continental W. Europe	Common Market	Other Four[1]	Rest of W. Europe	Other	Territories etc.[2]	Asia[3]	U.S.S.R.[4]	Latin America[5]
Britain ...	100	19.7	—	37.8	22.3	12.0	8.4	1.8	20.0	5.2	2.9	3.0	8.5
W. Germany ...	100	20.4	3.5	10.1	40.2	23.5	11.9	4.7	25.8	6.1	4.9	3.6	10.7
France	100	14.5	3.7	16.3	27.7	21.4	3.5	2.8	37.8	25.7	4.9	2.4	4.6
Italy	100	20.5	4.9	15.6	34.8	21.6	8.5	4.6	24.2	5.3	9.0	3.2	6.7
Belgium & Lux. ...	100	13.6	8.2	8.2	51.0	43.6	4.9	2.5	19.0	8.2	4.1	2.0	4.3
Netherlands ...	100	14.5	8.0	6.7	48.7	41.2	5.6	2.0	22.1	3.7	7.6	2.1	8.4
Common Market	100	17.0	5.2	11.7	39.2	28.4	7.3	3.5	27.0	10.7	5.9	2.8	7.4
Denmark ...	100	10.1	24.4	0.7	51.5	36.2	13.1	2.1	13.1	2.5	2.4	3.6	4.6
Norway ...	100	13.3	17.4	3.1	52.8	31.2	19.8	1.8	13.3	2.9	2.7	3.8	3.8
Sweden ...	100	13.4	13.8	4.9	50.4	39.4	8.5	2.5	17.5	3.5	3.4	3.5	7.2
Austria ...	100	13.3	4.2	3.6	61.0	52.0	2.4	6.7	18.0	3.5	1.7	10.4	2.4
Other Four ...	100	12.6	15.1	3.4	53.1	39.3	10.7	3.1	15.8	3.1	2.7	4.8	5.1
Common Market + Other Four	100	16.2	7.2	10.0	42.0	30.5	8.0	3.4	24.7	9.2	5.2	3.2	6.9

[1] Denmark, Norway, Sweden and Austria.
[2] Territories of Continental Western Europe, *plus* Morocco, Tunisia, Finland, Spain and Yugoslavia.
[3] Non-Sterling Middle Eastern and other Far Eastern Countries.
[4] U.S.S.R., Other Eastern European Countries and China.
[5] Dollar-plus-Non-Dollar Countries.

Source: U.N. Commodity Trace Statistics, Series D. Vol. VII, No. 4.

but proportions of the imports of Common Market countries ranging from 6½ per cent for the Netherlands to 16½ per cent for France, with an average of 11½ per cent. The rest of the Sterling Area supplied 3½ per cent of the imports of the 'other four'. Britain herself provided proportions of the imports of Common Market countries ranging from 3½ per cent of West German to 8 per cent of Belgian imports, but 15 per cent of the imports of the other four countries.

The U.S.A. and Canada provided 19½ per cent of British imports, and proportion of Europeans imports ranging from 10 per cent for Denmark to 20½ per cent for Italy and West Germany; 16 per cent of total European imports came from the U.S.A. and Canada.

The only other sources which did not supply a lower fraction of British than of European imports were the 'other four' and Latin America. The other four supplied 8½ per cent of British imports, and proportions of the Common Market countries' imports ranging from 3½ per cent for France to 12 per cent for West Germany, with an average of 7½ per cent. The other four supplied 10½ per cent of each others' imports.

For most other sources the European figures were higher than the British. Continental Western Europe supplied 22½ per cent of British imports, but proportions of Common Market countries' imports ranging from 27½ per cent of French to 51 per cent of Belgian imports, with an average of 39 per cent; and Europe supplied 53 per cent of the other four countries' imports. Both the Common Market countries and the rest of Western Europe (i.e. excluding the 'other four') contributed to this difference. The Common Market countries supplied 12 per cent of British imports, but they supplied proportions of each others' imports ranging from 21½ per cent for France and Italy to 43½ per cent for Belgium, with an average of 28½ per cent; and the Common Market countries supplied 39½ per cent of the imports of the 'other four' countries. The rest of Western Europe provided 2 per cent of British imports, but proportions of European imports ranging from 2 per cent of Norwegian to 6½ per cent of Austrian imports, with a European average of 3½ per cent.

Other countries—i.e. excluding the U.S.A. and Canada, the Sterling Area, and Continental Western Europe—provided 20 per cent of British imports, 27 per cent of Common Market countries', and 16 per cent of the other four countries' imports. Imports from the territories of Continental Western Europe *plus* Morocco, Tunisia, Spain, Finland and Yugoslavia formed 5 per cent of British imports; the proportion of imports from this group into European countries other than France ranged from 2½ per cent of Danish to 8 per cent of Belgian imports, but the French figure of 25½ per cent raised the European average for this group to 9 per cent.

The non-sterling Middle and Far East provided 3 per cent of British imports, but 6 per cent of Common Market countries' and 2½ per cent of the other four countries' imports. The U.S.S.R., Eastern Europe and

China provided 3 per cent of British and 3 per cent of the Common Market countries' imports, but 5 per cent of the imports of the other four. Latin America provided $8\frac{1}{2}$ per cent of British imports, and proportions of European imports ranging from $2\frac{1}{2}$ per cent of Austrian to $10\frac{1}{2}$ per cent of German imports, with a European average of 7 per cent.

II. THE COMMODITY COMPOSITION OF EUROPEAN TRADE IN 1957

Exports. Table 5 shows the commodity composition of exports in the first nine months of 1957 from Britain, the Common Market countries, and a further five European countries—Denmark, Norway, Sweden, Austria and Switzerland. Table 6 shows the derived percentage figures. The first major difference between the composition of British exports and those of the European countries is that all three groups of primary products —'food' (including beverages and tobacco), raw materials, and fuel— formed smaller proportions of British than of European exports, while the remaining classes combined—i.e. manufactured and semi-manufactured goods—accounted for a higher proportion of British than of European exports.

Thus while 6 per cent of British exports consisted of food, the proportions for the Common Market countries ranged from 2 per cent of West German to $27\frac{1}{2}$ per cent of Netherlands exports, with an average of 11 per cent; while the proportion of food in the exports of the other five ranged from 4 per cent of Austrian or Swedish to 62 per cent of Danish exports, with an average of 16 per cent. Raw materials formed 4 per cent of British exports, while for the Common Market countries the proportions ranged from $3\frac{1}{2}$ per cent of West German to 9 per cent of French exports, with an average of 6 per cent, and for the other five the proportions ranged from $2\frac{1}{2}$ per cent of Swiss to $38\frac{1}{2}$ per cent of Swedish exports, with an average of $20\frac{1}{2}$ per cent.

Fuel accounted for $4\frac{1}{2}$ per cent of British exports; for Common Market countries the proportions of exports consisting of fuel ranged from $5\frac{1}{2}$ per cent for France to 15 per cent for the Netherlands, with an average of 8 per cent, while the other five exported very little fuel, with an average of $\frac{1}{2}$ per cent.

Thus the remaining classes of exports, i.e. manufactures and semi-manufactures of various kinds, accounted for $85\frac{1}{2}$ per cent of British exports; for the Common Market countries the proportions ranged from 49 per cent for the Netherlands to $87\frac{1}{2}$ per cent of West German exports, with an average of 75 per cent; while for the other five the proportion of exports in these groups varied from 31 per cent of Danish to $91\frac{1}{2}$ per cent of Swiss exports, with an average of $62\frac{1}{2}$ per cent.

Arranging the various types of manufactured goods distinguished in order of their relative importance in British as compared with European exports, the list reads: transport equipment, metal-using manufactures,

TABLE 5.　*Commodity Composition of Exports in 1957 (1st 9 months).　U.S. $mn.*

From:	All Commodities	Food etc. (1)	Raw Materials (2)	Fuel (3)	All Other (4)	Chemicals (5)	Textiles (6)	Base Metals (7)	Metal-using Manufactures (8)	Transport Equipment (9)	Other (10)
Britain	6,957	417	264	323	5,953	563	642	657	2,000	1,089	1,002
W. Germany	6,264	118	212	464	5,470	669	239	837	2,020	825	879
France	3,755	531	344	215	2,665	307	324	563	484	375	613
Italy	1,874	440	82	134	1,218	117	252	118	278	201	252
Belgium and Luxemburg	2,380	86	181	154	1,959	164	252	783	276	100	384
Netherlands	2,263	620	194	340	1,109	193	166	143	279	93	234
Common Market	16,536	1,795	1,013	1,307	12,421	1,450	1,233	2,444	3,337	1,594	2,362
Denmark	837	521	55	1	260	26	11	15	122	33	54
Norway	606	112	151	3	340	51	4	144	22	44	76
Sweden	1,584	65	611	3	905	34	10	134	324	172	232
Austria	724	29	154	19	522	32	56	156	116	26	136
Switzerland	1,141	65	31	2	1,043	203	127	19	343	12	340
Other Five	4,892	792	1,002	28	3,070	346	208	468	927	287	838
Common Market+Other Five	21,428	2,587	2,015	1,335	15,491	1,796	1,441	2,912	4,264	1,881	3,200

Source: E.C.E. Economic Survey of Europe in 1958. A-16.

(1) Food, Beverages, and Tobacco. S.I.T.C. Sections 0 and 1.
(2) Raw Materials. S.I.T.C. Sections 2 and 4.
(3) Fuel. S.I.T.C. Section 3.
(4) All Other. All commodities less (1), (2) and (3).
(5) Chemicals. S.I.T.C. section 5.
(6) Textile yarns and manufactures (excluding clothing). S.I.T.C. div. 65.
(7) Base Metals. S.I.T.C. div. 68.
(8) Metal using manufactures (excluding transport equipment). S.I.T.C. divs. 69, 71 and 72.
(9) Transport Equipment. S.I.T.C. div. 73.
(10) Other S.I.T.C. Sections 8, 9; divisions 61 to 64, 66, and 67.

TABLE 6. *Commodity Composition of Exports in 1957.* (*1st 9 months.*) *Per cent.*

From:	Of:	All Commodities	Food etc. (1)	Raw Materials (2)	Fuel (3)	All Other (4)	Chemicals (5)	Textiles (6)	Base Metals (7)	Metal-using Manufactures (8)	Transport Equipment (9)	Other (10)
Britain	...	100	6.0	3.8	4.6	85.6	8.1	9.2	9.4	28.8	15.6	14.4
W. Germany	...	100	1.9	3.4	7.4	87.3	10.7	3.8	13.4	32.2	13.2	14.0
France	...	100	14.1	9.2	5.7	71.0	8.2	8.6	15.0	12.9	10.0	16.3
Italy	...	100	23.5	4.4	7.1	65.0	6.2	13.4	6.3	14.8	10.7	13.4
Belgium and Luxemburg	...	100	3.6	7.6	6.5	82.3	6.9	10.6	32.9	11.6	4.2	16.1
Netherlands	...	100	27.4	8.6	15.0	49.0	8.5	7.3	6.3	12.3	4.1	10.3
Common Market	...	100	10.8	6.1	7.9	75.0	8.8	7.5	14.8	20.2	9.6	14.3
Denmark	...	100	62.2	6.6	0.1	31.1	3.1	1.3	1.8	14.6	3.9	6.5
Norway	...	100	18.5	24.9	0.5	56.1	8.4	0.7	23.8	3.6	7.3	12.5
Sweden	...	100	4.1	38.6	0.2	57.1	2.1	0.6	8.5	20.4	10.8	14.6
Austria	...	100	4.0	21.3	2.6	72.1	4.4	7.7	21.6	16.0	3.6	18.8
Switzerland	...	100	5.7	2.7	0.2	91.4	17.8	11.1	1.7	30.0	1.1	29.8
Other Five	...	100	16.2	20.5	0.6	62.7	7.1	4.3	9.6	18.9	5.9	17.1
Common Market + Other Five	...	100	12.1	9.4	6.2	72.2	8.4	6.7	13.6	19.9	8.8	14.9

Source: E.C.E. Economic Survey of Europe in 1958. A-16.

(1) Food, Beverages, and Tobacco. S.I.T.C. Sections 0 and 1.
(2) Raw Materials. S.I.T.C. Sections 2 and 4.
(3) Fuel. S.I.T.C. Section 3.
(4) All Other. All commodities less (1), (2) and (3).
(5) Chemicals. S.I.T.C. section 5.
(6) Textile yarns and manufactures (excluding clothing). S.I.T.C. div. 65.
(7) Base Metals. S.I.T.C. div. 68.
(8) Metal using manufactures (excluding transport equipment). S.I.T.C. divs. 69, 71 and 72.
(9) Transport Equipment. S.I.T.C. div. 73.
(10) Other S.I.T.C. Sections 8, 9; divisions 61 to 64, 66, and 67.

and textiles, above average; and other goods, chemicals and base metals below average.

Transport equipment formed 15½ per cent of British exports; for Common Market countries the proportion ranged from 4 per cent of Netherlands to 13 per cent of West German exports, with an average of 9½ per cent; while for the other five the proportions ranged from 1 per cent of Swiss to 11 per cent of Swedish exports, with an average of 6 per cent.

Metal-using manufactures formed 29 per cent of British exports; for the Common Market countries the proportion ranged from 11½ per cent of Belgian to 32 per cent of West German exports; with an average of 20 per cent, and for the other five the proportion ranged from 3½ per cent of Norwegian to 30 per cent of Swiss exports, with an average of 19 per cent.

Textiles formed 9 per cent of British exports; for Common Market countries the proportions ranged from 4 per cent of West German to 13½ per cent of Italian exports, with an average of 7½ per cent; and for the other five the proportions of textiles in total exports ranged from ½ per cent of Swedish to 11 per cent of Swiss exports, with an average of 4½ per cent.

Other goods formed 14½ per cent of British exports: the proportions for Common Market countries ranged from 10½ per cent of Netherlands to 16½ per cent of French exports, with an average of 14½ per cent, and for the other five the proportions ranged from 6½ per cent of Danish to 30 per cent of Swiss exports, with an average of 17 per cent.

Chemicals formed 8 per cent of British exports: for Common Market countries the proportions ranged from 6 per cent of Italian to 10½ per cent of West German exports, with an average of 9 per cent; and for the other five the proportions ranged from 2 per cent of Swedish to 18 per cent of Swiss exports, with an average of 7 per cent.

Base metals, finally, formed 9½ per cent of British exports: the proportions for Common Market countries ranged from 6½ per cent of Netherlands to 33 per cent of Belgian exports, with an average of 15 per cent; while for the other five the proportion ranged from 1½ per cent of Swiss to 24 per cent of Norwegian exports, with an average of 9½ per cent.

Imports. Table 7 shows the commodity composition of imports in the first nine months of 1957, and Table 8 the derived percentages.

Food formed a higher proportion, 36½ per cent, of British imports than of those of any other country shown. For Common Market countries the proportion of imports consisting of food ranged from 12½ per cent of Italian to 27 per cent of West German imports, with an average of 19½ per cent; while for the other five the proportions ranged from 11½ per cent of Norwegian to 19 per cent of Swiss imports, with an average of 14½ per cent.

Raw materials formed 29 per cent of British imports; this figure is higher than that for Europe as a whole, chiefly because of the lesser

TABLE 7. Commodity Composition of Imports in 1957. (1st 9 months.) U.S. $mn.

From:	Of:	All Commodities	Food etc. (1)	Raw Materials (2)	Fuel (3)	All Other (4)	Chemicals (5)	Textiles (6)	Base Metals (7)	Metal-using Manufactures (8)	Transport Equipment (9)	Other (10)
Britain	...	8,666	3,177	2,508	1,012	1,969	236	184	570	348	92	540
W. Germany ...	...	5,526	1,487	1,750	653	1,636	164	268	491	237	93	382
France	...	4,774	1,005	1,384	962	1,423	195	51	321	513	87	255
Italy	...	2,711	345	960	583	823	134	40	217	278	37	118
Belgium and Luxemburg	...	2,581	350	605	337	1,289	150	99	211	327	161	342
Netherlands ...	...	3,079	439	516	536	1,588	148	168	299	460	164	348
Common Market ...	...	18,671	3,626	5,215	3,071	6,759	791	626	1,539	1,815	542	1,445
Denmark	...	1,008	140	116	188	564	83	74	111	115	88	92
Norway	...	966	109	77	114	666	47	62	128	137	222	71
Sweden	...	1,815	229	121	360	1,105	97	121	209	291	182	204
Austria	...	832	132	150	123	427	57	58	45	141	58	70
Switzerland ...	...	1,493	282	175	151	885	125	71	203	202	95	187
Other Five	...	6,114	892	639	936	3,647	409	386	696	886	645	624
Common Market + Other Five ...		24,785	4,518	5,854	4,007	10,406	1,200	1,012	2,235	2,701	1,187	2,069

Source: E.C.E. Economic Survey of Europe in 1958. A-16.
(1) Food, Beverages, and Tobacco. S.I.T.C. Sections 0 and 1.
(2) Raw Materials. S.I.T.C. Sections 2 and 4.
(3) Fuel. S.I.T.C. Section 3.
(4) All Other. All commodities less (1), (2) and (3).
(5) Chemicals. S.I.T.C. section 5.
(6) Textile yarns and manufactures (excluding clothing). S.I.T.C. div. 65.
(7) Base Metals. S.I.T.C. div. 68.
(8) Metal using manufactures (excluding transport equipment). S.I.T.C. divs. 69, 71 and 72.
(9) Transport Equipment. S.I.T.C. div. 73.
(10) Other S.I.T.C. Sections 8, 9; divisions 61 to 64, 66, and 67.

importance of raw materials in the other five countries' imports; these showed proportions ranging from $6\frac{1}{2}$ per cent of Swedish to 18 per cent of Austrian imports, with an average of $10\frac{1}{2}$ per cent. For the Common Market countries the proportion of imports consisting of raw materials varied from 17 per cent of Netherlands to $35\frac{1}{2}$ per cent of Italian imports, with an average of 28 per cent, very close to the British figure.

Fuel formed $11\frac{1}{2}$ per cent of British imports, a lower figure than the European average of 16 per cent; for the Common Market countries the proportion of total imports consisting of fuel ranged from 12 per cent of West German to $21\frac{1}{2}$ per cent of Italian imports, with an average of $16\frac{1}{2}$ per cent, while for the other five the proportion ranged from 10 per cent of Swiss to 20 per cent of Swedish imports, with an average of $15\frac{1}{2}$ per cent.

The result of these differences for the three classes of primary commodities combined was to leave all other products—i.e. manufactured and semi-manufactured goods —forming $22\frac{1}{2}$ per cent of British imports, a lower proportion than that for any other country shown. For Common Market countries the proportion of imports consisting of manufactures ranged from $29\frac{1}{2}$ per cent of W. German to $51\frac{1}{2}$ per cent of Netherlands imports, with an average of 36 per cent; while for the other five the proportions ranged from $51\frac{1}{2}$ per cent of Austrian to 68 per cent of Norwegian imports, with an average of $59\frac{1}{2}$ per cent.

The lesser share of manufactures in British, as compared with total European imports, is common to all the classes of imports of manufactures distinguished in Table 8, but it is most marked in transport equipment and metal-using manufactures, while textiles and chemicals are near to the average, and there is least difference between Britain and Europe in the proportion of imports consisting of base metals and other goods.

Transport equipment formed only 1 per cent of British imports; while for the Common Market countries the proportions ranged from $1\frac{1}{2}$ per cent of Italian to 6 per cent of Belgian imports, with an average of 3 per cent; and for the other five the proportions ranged from $6\frac{1}{2}$ per cent of Swiss to 23 per cent of Norwegian imports, with an average of $10\frac{1}{2}$ per cent.

Metal-using manufactures formed 4 per cent of British imports: for Common Market countries the proportions ranged from $4\frac{1}{2}$ per cent of W. German to 15 per cent of Netherlands imports, with an average of $9\frac{1}{2}$ per cent; and for the other five the proportions ranged from $11\frac{1}{2}$ per cent of Danish to 17 per cent of Austrian imports, with an average of $14\frac{1}{2}$ per cent.

Textiles formed 2 per cent of British imports; for the Common Market countries the proportions varied from 1 per cent of French to $5\frac{1}{2}$ per cent of Netherlands imports, with an average of $3\frac{1}{2}$ per cent, and for the other five the proportions ranged from 5 per cent of Swiss to $7\frac{1}{2}$ per cent of Danish imports, with an average of $6\frac{1}{2}$ per cent.

Chemicals formed $2\frac{1}{2}$ per cent of British imports; for the common Market countries the proportions ranged from 3 per cent of W. German to

TABLE 8. *Commodity Composition of Imports in 1957.* (*1st 9 months.*) *Per cent.*

From:	Of:	All Commodities	Food etc. (1)	Raw Materials (2)	Fuel (3)	All Other (4)	Chemicals (5)	Textiles (6)	Base Metals (7)	Metal-using Manufactures (8)	Transport Equipment (9)	Other (10)
Britain	...	100	36.6	29.0	11.7	22.7	2.7	2.1	6.6	4.0	1.1	6.2
W. Germany ...	...	100	26.9	31.7	11.8	29.6	3.0	4.8	8.9	4.3	1.7	6.9
France	...	100	21.0	29.0	20.2	29.8	4.1	1.1	6.7	10.7	1.8	5.3
Italy	...	100	12.7	35.4	21.5	30.4	4.9	1.5	8.0	10.3	1.4	4.4
Belgium and Luxemburg ...	...	100	13.5	23.4	13.0	49.9	5.8	3.8	8.2	12.7	6.2	13.2
Netherlands	...	100	14.2	16.8	17.4	51.5	4.8	5.5	9.7	14.9	5.3	11.3
Common Market	...	100	19.4	28.0	16.5	36.2	4.2	3.4	8.2	9.7	2.9	7.7
Denmark	...	100	13.9	11.5	18.6	56.0	8.2	7.3	11.0	11.4	8.7	9.1
Norway	...	100	11.3	8.0	11.8	68.0	4.9	6.4	13.2	14.2	23.0	7.3
Sweden	...	100	12.6	6.7	19.8	60.8	5.3	6.7	11.5	16.0	10.0	11.2
Austria	...	100	15.9	18.0	14.8	51.3	6.9	7.0	5.4	17.0	7.0	8.4
Switzerland ...	...	100	18.9	11.7	10.1	59.2	8.4	4.8	13.6	13.5	6.4	12.5
Other Five	...	100	14.6	10.4	15.3	59.7	6.7	6.3	11.4	14.5	10.5	10.2
Common Market + Other Five ...	...	100	18.2	23.6	16.2	42.0	4.8	4.1	9.0	10.9	4.8	8.4

Source: E.C.E. Economic Survey of Europe in 1958. A-16.
(1) Food, Beverages, and Tobacco. S.I.T.C. Sections 0 and 1.
(2) Raw Materials. S.I.T.C. Sections 2 and 4.
(3) Fuel. S.I.T.C. Section 3.
(4) All Other. All commodities less (1), (2) and (3).
(5) Chemicals. S.I.T.C. section 5.
(6) Textile yarns and manufactures (excluding clothing). S.I.T.C. div. 65.
(7) Base Metals. S.I.T.C. div. 68.
(8) Metal using manufactures (excluding transport equipment). S.I.T.C. divs. 69, 71 and 72.
(9) Transport Equipment. S.I.T.C. div. 73.
(10) Other S.I.T.C. Sections 8, 9; divisions 61 to 64, 66, and 67.

6 per cent of Belgian imports, with an average of 4 per cent; and for the other five the proportions ranged from 5 per cent of Norwegian to 8½ per cent of Swiss imports, with an average of 6½ per cent.

Base metals formed 6½ per cent of British imports. For the Common Market countries the proportions ranged from 6¼ per cent of French to 9½ per cent of Netherlands imports, with an average of 8 per cent; and for the other five the proportions ranged from 5½ per cent of Austrian to 13½ per cent of Swiss imports, with an average of 11½ per cent.

Other goods, finally, formed 6 per cent of British imports: for the Common Market countries the proportions ranged from 4½ per cent of Italian to 13 per cent of Belgian imports, with an average of 7½ per cent; while for the other five the proportions ranged from 7½ per cent of Norwegian to 12½ per cent of Swiss imports, with an average of 10 per cent.

III. RECENT DEVELOPMENTS IN THE EUROPEAN ECONOMIES

Rate of Growth. Table 9 shows various indices of economic growth since 1953 for Britain and various European countries. Most of the figures refer to 1958, but in some cases the 1958 figure was not available, and in others the temporary recession had led to the 1958 figure lying below an earlier one, in which case to avoid a pessimistic bias the highest year—usually 1957—has been used. The four indices taken are Gross National Product, Industrial Production, Gross Domestic Fixed Capital Formation, and Output per Man-hour in Industry. All are real measures with 1953 = 100. Each of the four series shows that Britain has been growing more slowly than any of the Common Market countries, or Austria, and more slowly than the (unweighted) average of the ' other four ' (Denmark, Norway, Sweden and Austria).

For Gross National Product the index for Britain was 112—only Denmark, of all the countries shown, grew more slowly with 109 (in 1957); the average for the other four was 121, and the Common Market countries showed indices ranging from 113 for Belgium to 138 for W. Germany, with an average (weighting W. Germany 3, France 3, Italy 2, Belgium 1, Netherlands 1) of 128.

In Industrial Production Britain, at 116 (in 1957) comes lowest. The other four countries average 128, and the Common Market countries, with Belgium at 123 again in the rear and France at 154 in the lead, average 144. In Gross Domestic Fixed Capital Formation Britain at 128 does better than the Scandinavian countries, but worse than Austria or than any of the Common Market countries, which with Belgium at 129 in the rear and W. Germany at 151 in the van, show an average of 145.

Finally, to show that the other divergencies do not result merely from different rates of expansion, or changes in the composition, of the labour force, we take Output per man-hour (in Norway and Sweden, per man) in Industry. Here again Britain at 110 comes bottom of the list. The other

TABLE 9

Indicators of Economic Growth since 1953
Volume Indices for 1958 (except where indicated) with 1953=100.

	Gross National Product	Industrial Production	Gross Domestic Fixed Capital Formation	Output per Man-hour in Industry
Britain	112	116[1]	128	110
W. Germany	138	151	151	133
France	127	154	150	140
Italy	127	140	139[1]	135
Belgium	113[1]	123[1]	129[2]	128
Netherlands	123	126	139[1]	119
Common Market[3] ...	128	144	145	133
Denmark	109[4]	118	107[5]	114
Norway	115[1]	126[1]	122	121[6]
Sweden	119	119	124	117[6]
Austria	142	150	178	124
Other Four[7]	121	128	133	119

Sources: G.N.P.: O.E.E.C. *Policies for Sound Economic Growth*, p. 103. Industrial Production: E.C.E. *Economic Survey of Europe in 1958*, II–5. Capital Formation: O.E.E.C. *Policies for Sound Economic Growth*, p. 105. Output per Man-hour in Industry: E.C.E. *Economic Survey of Europe in 1958*, A–8.

[1] 1957 figure.
[2] 1956 figure (1958 not available).
[3] Average weighted W. Germany 3, France 3, Italy 2, Belgium 1, Netherlands 1.
[4] 1957 figure; 1958 figure not available.
[5] 1954 figure; 1958 figure not available.
[6] Output per worker; output per man-hour not available.
[7] Unweighted average.

four show an average of 119, and the Common Market countries, with the Netherlands at 119 in the rear, and France at 140 in the lead, average 133.

Thus it is apparent that on any of these indicators Britain has been lagging behind the rest of W. Europe, over a five-year period which can fairly be held to post-date the recovery from the effects of the last War. While it is not appropriate to attempt to forecast here exactly when recovery from the present slight recession will take place, there appears to be no reason why the next few years should not see a further expansion of the European countries as fast as in the period discussed, for quite apart from any stimulating effects of the Common Market itself, there is a high rate of investment, a continued growth of population is expected, and the supply prospects of raw materials are good, so that it is hard to see any real bottlenecks arising.

Trade and National Incomes. Table 10 shows the proportions of exports and imports to Gross National Product for various European countries for the years 1953 to 1957. This shows that for no country has there been any apparent tendency for foreign trade to fall in proportion

TABLE 10

Trade as per cent of Gross National Product

		1953	1954	1955	1956	1957	Average
Britain	Exports	15.9	15.4	15.8	16.0	15.8	15.8
	Imports	19.7	18.7	20.3	18.7	18.6	19.2
W. Germany	Exports	12.8	14.3	14.6	15.9	17.1[1]	14.9*
	Imports	11.0	12.5	13.9	14.4	15.0[1]	13.4*
France	Exports	8.9	9.3	10.1	8.5	9.1	9.2
	Imports	9.2	9.4	9.7	10.5	10.9	9.9*
Italy	Exports	8.1	8.2	8.5	9.2	10.1	8.8*
	Imports	13.0	12.2	12.4	13.6	14.5	13.1
Belgium and Lux.	Exports	26.2	25.5	29.1	30.8	29.6	28.2*
	Imports	28.0	28.1	29.7	31.9	31.9	29.9*
Netherlands	Exports	33.7	33.8	34.1	33.8	33.6	33.8
	Imports	37.2	40.0	40.7	44.0	44.5	41.3*
Denmark	Exports	23.4	24.0	25.5	25.0	24.7	24.5
	Imports	26.1	29.2	28.4	29.4	28.6	28.3
Norway	Exports	17.6	18.7	19.1	20.7	20.8	19.4*
	Imports	31.6	32.7	33.0	32.5	32.3	32.4
Sweden	Exports	19.4	19.6	19.7	20.6	21.0	20.1*
	Imports	20.7	22.0	22.8	23.4	23.9	22.6*
Austria	Exports	17.0	18.1	18.1	20.0	20.9	18.8*
	Imports	17.1	19.4	23.0	22.9	24.1	21.3*

Source: I.M.F. *International Financial Statisitcs*, April 1959, National Tables.

* Indicates increasing trend.

[1] W. German figures for 1958: exports 16.6 per cent, imports 13.9 per cent of G.N.P.

TABLE 11

The Cost of Living (1953=100)

	1954	1955	1956	1957	1958
Britain	102	106	112	115	119
W. Germany	100	102	105	106	110
France	100	101	103	106	121
Italy	103	105	109	110	113
Belgium and Luxemburg	101	101	104	107	108
Netherlands	104	106	108	115	117
Common Market[1]	101	102½	105½	108	114½
Common Market without France ...	101½	103	106½	108½	111½
Denmark	100	105	110	114	119
Norway	104	105	109	112	117
Sweden	101	104	109	113	119
Austria	103	105	108	112	114
Other Four[2]	102	105	109	113	117

Source: I.M.F. *International Financial Statistics*, April 1959.

[1] Common Market average with weights W. Germany 3, France 3, Italy 2, Belgium and Luxemburg, 1, Netherlands 1.   Without France, same weights omitting France.

[2] Unweighted average.

C

TABLE 12

Gold and Foreign Exchange Holdings
(U.S. $mn. at end of year)

	1953	1954	1955	1956	1957	1958
Britain	2,564	2,798	2,156	2,172	2,374	3,069
W. Germany	1,532	2,147	2,555	3,603	4,634	5,048
France	956	1,369	2,076	1,356	775	1,055
Italy	952	1,041	1,237	1,308	1,532	2,263
Belgium and Lux. ...	838	858	944	946	995	1,348
Netherlands	1,004	1,108	1,108	959	974	1,370
Common Market ...	5,282	6,523	7,920	8,172	8,910	11,084
Denmark	167	143	135	131	172	209
Norway	143	138	165	179	184	246
Sweden	374	430	456	463	445	471
Austria	269	360	359	403	499	659
Other Four	953	1,071	1,115	1,176	1,300	1,585

Source: O.E.E.C. *Policies for Sound Economic Growth*, p. 62.

to Gross National Product, while for several countries, particularly W. Germany and Austria, there has been a very marked increase (though the 1958 figures available for W. Germany show a slight fall in the proportion of trade to G.N.P.). Belgium and Sweden show the same tendency to increasing participation in trade to a lesser extent; exports but not imports have shown a rising trend in Italy and Norway, and imports but not exports in France and the Netherlands. Britain has consistently shown a higher dependence on foreign trade than France, Italy or W. Germany, but less than any of the other countries shown.

Prices. One factor affecting the results of closer trading links between countries is the relative movement of their price levels. Table 11 shows the changes in the cost-of-living indices of Britain and various European countries since 1953 (with 1953=100). Only France showed a rise, to 121, greater than that for Britain of 119, while in Denmark and Sweden the rise was the same as in Britain. The index for the Common Market countries rose to $114\frac{1}{2}$; but as France has devalued during the period, it is pertinent to consider the index for the other Common Market countries; until 1957 omitting France hardly alters the index, but for 1958 the other Common Market countries' average was $111\frac{1}{2}$, showing that Britain's inflation was $1\frac{1}{2}$ points per year faster over the period.

Gold and Foreign Exchange Reserves. If European production and incomes continue to grow, and trade continues to increase in proportion, or a little more than in proportion, then there will be an increased need for gold and foreign exchange reserves as a backing for this trade; the need for reserves will be further increased if the price-increases continue, and if the new monetary arrangements replacing the European Payments Union, and the elimination of tariffs and quotas within Europe, lead to yet further

TABLE 13

Gold and Foreign Exchange Holdings relative to Imports
(*Gold and foreign exchange holdings at end of year as per cent of imports during year*)

	1953	1954	1955	1956	1957	1958*	Average
Britain	27	30	20	20	21	29	24
W. Germany ...	40	47	44	54	61	70	53
France	23	31	44	24	13	18	25
Italy	40	43	46	41	42	72	47
Belgium and Lux.	35	34	33	29	29	44	34
Netherlands ...	43	39	34	26	24	39	34
Common Market ...	35	39	41	36	36	49	39
Denmark ...	17	12	11	10	13	16	13
Norway	16	13	15	15	14	19	15
Sweden	24	24	23	21	18	21	22
Austria	49	55	40	41	44	61	49
Other Four ...	24	23	22	21	21	27	23

Sources: O.E.E.C. *Policies for Sound Economic Growth*, pp. 59 and 120.
* Based on Annual Rate of Imports over first 9 months.

increases in trade, with no provision of automatic short-term financial assistance for countries in payments difficulties. Table 12 shows the gold and foreign exchange holdings of Britain and various European countries at the end of each year from 1953 to 1958. This shows that, while every country finished 1958 with foreign exchange reserves larger than those held at the end of 1953, this was in some cases entirely due to gains made in 1958, which was a good year for every country's reserves: Britain, France and the Netherlands had lost reserves over the previous four years. The countries which showed a persistent tendency to gain reserves were W. Germany, Italy, Belgium, Norway, Sweden and Austria. Over the whole period half the total of British and European gains of reserves went to W. Germany.

The actual reserves need to be compared with the transactions they are required to finance, however; and Table 13 shows end-of-year reserves as a percentage of total imports during the year. This can be treated as an index of the adequacy of reserves (necessarily imperfect, as there are other current and capital transactions to be backed by reserves, as well as visible trade). The only country which on this criterion has shown a clear tendency to increasing adequacy of reserves, even including the all-round gains of 1958, is W. Germany.

Merton College
Oxford

EUROPEAN ECONOMIC COMMUNITY AND THE FREE TRADE AREA NEGOTIATIONS, 1956–1958

By G. D. N. Worswick

At the end of 1956, the six ' Schumann Plan ' countries, which had already formed the European Coal and Steel Community in 1951, had decided to go further towards establishing a European Economic Community which would incorporate a Customs Union, or Common Market, whereby trade in industrial goods between members would be freed from quota restrictions and from all tariffs and there would be a common tariff against goods from outside countries. There was to be a parallel move to free trade in agricultural products, but a special regime would have to be worked out for them.

The creation of such a customs union, or common market, by the Six countries obviously confronted non-member countries with the possibility that they might be put at a disadvantage in selling goods to any member of the common market in competition with other members of that market.

In April 1956 the Six themselves had put forward the idea that the customs union might be accompanied by free trade area arrangements with certain other countries and in July 1956 the Council of O.E.E.C. set up a Working Party to study possible forms and methods of such association. In the course of a debate in the House of Commons on November 26th, the British Government explained that, following consultation with other Commonwealth Governments, they had concluded that it was desirable and consistent both with their Commonwealth relationships and with their other international obligations to enter into negotiations for the establishment of an *industrial* free trade area in Europe.

This was the position when the *Symposium* which forms the first part of this book was written. In January 1957 the O.E.E.C. Working Party reported that it was technically possible to operate a free trade area in Europe which would include the customs and economic union of the Six, and the stage was set for the opening of formal negotiations to this end, and they were duly inaugurated by a resolution of the Ministerial Council of O.E.E.C. on February 12th–13th, 1957.

Those negotiations continued until November 14th, 1958, when an announcement was made to the Press on behalf of the French Government that it did not seem possible to them to establish the free trade area as it had been proposed and that they were looking for a new solution. Doubts had been expressed by the French from the earliest days, but the nature and timing of this announcement were such as to lead to the suspension of work by the inter-Governmental Committee of the O.E.E.C. countries, which had been steering the negotiations.

In the event, therefore, the first stage of the Common Market programme of tariff reduction and the removal of discrimination, particularly in import quotas, between members came into force on January 1st, 1959, without being accompanied by any similar multilateral moves in an associated Free Trade Area. Before we discuss the free trade area negotiations, and the consequences of their breakdown, it would be appropriate to take up the development of the European Economic Community itself, since the end of 1956.

THE EUROPEAN ECONOMIC COMMUNITY

The Treaty, or rather Treaties, of Rome signed by the Six on March 25th, 1957, established the European Economic Community and the European Atomic Energy Community. This book is mainly concerned with the questions of tariff and quota reduction, which are important aims of the Economic Community, but they are only a part of a broader objective of economic ' integration '. In a sense the aims of the Rome Treaty are unlimited. The signatories agree to establish an institutional machinery whose work could only be said to be completed when the economies of the Six became *one*, in the sense in which one talks of the British economy, or the U.S. economy. This theme is explicitly stated in the introduction to the first General Report of the Commission of the European Economic Community.

' Wherever the Treaty is applied, whether in general economic policy, in monetary policy, in policy relating to economic trends, in energy policy, in social or agricultural or transport policy, or in the policy governing economic relations with the associated overseas countries, the Community must be the expression of a policy consciously intended to be European.'

And again: ' If European integration is to make fresh advances it must become a reality both in practice and in the will of the individual.'

There is little doubt that this strain of almost mystical fervour is uncongenial to British statesmen, administrators and economists when they deal with economic and political negotiations. It is unlikely that they will be persuaded to share it. But it is possible that in their distaste for this kind of thing they failed to recognise its existence as a factor in the situation, and that this failure was a contributory cause of the ultimate breakdown of negotiations.

A most important new departure occurred at Brussels in February 1957 when the Six decided to associate their overseas territories within the Customs Union. The exact status of these territories will vary. Algeria and the Overseas Departments of France, for example, will be treated as full members of the Community but will be temporarily exempted from some provisions of the Treaty. Moreover, the Rome Treaty explicitly recognises the need for tariff and other protection of underdeveloped countries. Thus, while from January 1st, 1959, the Community countries have been required to cut customs duties on products from overseas territories by 10 per cent, the equivalent cut by the majority of overseas territories may be dispensed with for development, industrialisation or fiscal needs. The details are still being worked out. The implications of this step were perhaps less significant for Britain than for the Commonwealth countries.

An Overseas Countries Development Fund has also been set up by the Community, to which for an initial experimental period of five years the member countries have contributed the equivalent of $581 million which will be used for social projects such as schools, technical colleges and hospitals and also for economic development.

Of the two Rome Treaties signed on March 25th, 1957, to establish the European Economic Community and the European Atomic Community it is with the first that we are primarily concerned, but we should not overlook the fact that in the eyes of their promoters these ' communities ', as well as the Coal and Steel Community already established in 1951, are conceived as parts of a grand plan of ' integration '. Both treaties were duly ratified by the Six, and came into force on January 1st, 1958. As regards the former the year 1958 was mainly one the beginning of establishment of the institutions and organs of the Community.

The Council of Ministers, consisting of one member from each Government, with the task of securing co-ordination of economic policy, has begun to meet at monthly intervals.

The European Commission, the executive organ of the Treaty, composed of nine independent members (not more than two from any one country) has been appointed. This Commission does not have powers of enforcement similar to those of the High Authority of E.C.S.C.

The Parliamentary Assembly of 142 members, drawn from the Parliaments of the Six, and which replaces the Common Assembly of E.C.S.C., held its first session in March 1958, and met again in June, mainly to discuss the General Reports of E.C.S.C. The main purpose of the Assembly is to provide a forum for discussion.

Agreement has been reached among members on the composition of the new *Court of Justice,* which also will replace the Court of Justice of E.C.S.C.

The 101 members of the *Economic and Social Committee,* a special consultative committee of ' experts ' whose advice must, in certain cases, be heard by the Council and the Commission, were named and the Committee has met, being concerned so far with procedural questions. The Committee's membership includes prominent industrialists and commercial leaders, trade unionists, lawyers, and technical and economic experts.

Comment on the working of these organs would be premature: the same may be said of the European Investment Bank, beyond observing that it has been established and that in March 1959 its first loan was announced, of $24 million for three industrial and electrical power schemes in Italy and one in Luxembourg, the latter being a new scheme designed to be of use also to neighbouring Community countries.

Throughout 1958 detailed preparations were being made for the first stage of the ' opening of the markets ' whose ultimate aim is complete freedom of movement of goods, capital and persons within the Community. On January 1st, 1959, customs duties on all goods were cut by 10 per cent. At the same time all bilateral quotas were transformed into global quotas, whose total was 20 per cent above the total of quotas for 1958. There was a minimum quota increase of 10 per cent for each product, and in addition all quotas amounting to less than 3 per cent of national production were raised to the minimum of 3 per cent.[1] These cuts, as has already been mentioned, applied to the overseas territories, but only in certain cases have there been reciprocal tariff reductions by overseas countries, whose right to retain tariff protection for certain purposes is safeguarded by the Treaty.

The tariff reductions and quota increases apply also to agricultural goods, but during the transition period (12 years) there is a qualification, namely that each country can reduce or suspend imports from other Community countries if their prices fall below certain specified minimum levels. The Economic Commission is required, by December 31st, 1959, to submit proposals for the working out of a common agricultural policy for the Community.

We must be on our guard against concluding from this bald description of the successive stages in the creation of the European Economic Community that the whole business has hitherto been and will continue to be plain sailing. Close study of both the working of E.C.S.C., or of the negotiations for a Free Trade Area, remind us that the gap between intention and performance is often wide indeed. Following the French Government's announcement in November 1958 which precipitated the end of the O.E.E.C. negotiations, *The Times* carried a leader with the title ' France the Wrecker '. Following this line of thought it might be pertinent to ask whether the Economic Community itself might not founder once the full implications of its proposals come to be seen in practice. But it would seem wiser to continue to take for granted that the Community will ultimately become a reality.

---

[1] The main provisions for the abolition of tariffs are: The basic length of the transition period is 12 years. The transition period is divided into three stages of four years each. No duties may be raised or new ones introduced after January 1st, 1958. Ten per cent reduction of *each* duty in the first year; 10 per cent global reduction at each subsequent reduction, with a minimum of 5 per cent for each duty: 10 per cent reduction of each duty at each reduction for duties higher than 30 per cent.

THE FREE TRADE AREA NEGOTIATIONS

The successive steps in the creation of the Common Market were being followed at the same time as the negotiations for an associated Free Trade Area, which extended from the end of 1956 for the two following years. Towards the end of those negotiations the situation had been reached when, on major points, there was a tendency to seek first an agreed position for the Six before discussion with other O.E.E.C. members, and this was a factor making for delay from time to time in the Free Trade Area negotiations. There is, however, no evidence that the other members of the Community were consulted before the issue of the French Government's statement in November 1958 which precipitated the crisis in the negotiations.

The original British Free Trade Area proposals were strictly limited to the freeing of trade in industrial goods: moreover while trade within the Area should be free of restrictions, it was to be open to members of the Area (the Six to count in effect as one member from this point of view) to vary their tariffs with the rest of the world as they pleased (subject, of course, to any wider international obligations, e.g. under G.A.T.T.).

The association of such an Area with the Common Market had been pronounced as ' technically possible ' as early as January 1957 by a Working Party of O.E.E.C. In February 1957 three further working parties were established to investigate: (1) the technical details of freeing trade, (2) the arrangements to be made for agriculture, and (3) the special problems of under-developed countries (in effect, Turkey, Greece, Portugal, Eire and Iceland).

It was not until October 1957, however, that one can say that negotiations were decisively entered into. The delay was caused by the desire of the French, supported by the Germans, to secure the ratification of the Rome Treaty before engaging fully in Free Trade Area discussions. In October the O.E.E.C. Council ' declared its determination to secure the establishment of a European Free Trade Area which would comprise all member countries of the Organization; which would associate, on a multilateral basis, the European Economic Community with the other member countries and which, taking fully into consideration the objectives of the European Economic Community, would in practice take effect parallel with the Treaty of Rome '. At the same time the Council set up, to carry on the detailed negotiations, an inter-governmental committee at Ministerial level, under the Chairmanship of Mr. Maudling, Paymaster General, who had been appointed as special co-ordinator within the United Kingdom Government on free trade area questions.

It is the British Government's contention that already by October 1957 it had moved a long way from its initial position of desiring to confine discussion to removing barriers to trade in industrial goods. Her Majesty's

Government had 'gladly modified their original attitude' and were prepared to allow negotiations to cover virtually the whole range of subjects covered by the Rome Treaty, including agriculture.[1] It is arguable, however, that at the time the British Government were still deriving their inspiration from laissez-fair premises, and were only paying reluctant lip-service to ideas of 'harmonisation' and 'co-ordination'. Be that as it may, the French representative still described the free trade area as a project 'fraught with risks and uncertainties', and only four months later the French Government produced a memorandum proposing a completely different 'sector' approach to the liberalisation of trade.

A stage-by-stage account of the negotiations is indeed fascinating, prompting speculation whether in fact there was at any point a real hope of the negotiations reaching an agreed outcome. But there is already available the official British account, accompanied by a Blue Book containing the principal documents,[2] as well as an excellent description of the negotiations by Dr. Miriam Camps.[3] What will be attempted here, therefore, is simply a summary of what appear to have been the main points at issue.

The question of origin

Under the Treaty of Rome the Six will ultimately have a common tariff, while the associate members of the Free Trade Area would have tariffs of their own fixing, which for any commodity might be higher or lower than that of the Six, and which might be changed from time to time, subject of course to any other international obligations. These differences might lead to 'deflection' of trade, e.g. a commodity would enter country A, with a low tariff, and be re-exported duty free to one of the Six, thereby getting under the common tariff. That such deflections might well occur is clear, though it is not so easy to predict how extensive they would be or in what way they would necessarily be harmful. There is, indeed, an implicit assumption, most notably stressed by the French, that any deflection or 'distortion' of competition which has its origin in such tariff differences is harmful, in some general sense. This is not a necessary truth. Competition among enterprises in European countries is not so perfect that the only 'distortion' arises from tariff differences, whether on raw materials or final products. There are dozens of other kinds of distortion and there is therefore no certainty that the elimination of this particular one would be to the general advantage. It is worth mentioning this point because one does have the suspicion that lurking beneath many of the arguments for harmonization there is the perfectionism of a Walra-

[1] *Negotiations for a Free Trade Area*, Cmnd. 648, January 1959, para. 35.

[2] *Negotiations for a Free Trade Area.* Report on the Course of Negotiations, Cmnd. 648, and Documents Relating to the Negotiations, Cmnd. 641.

[3] *History of the Free Trade Area Negotiations.* P.E.P. April 1959. This paper, published as a *Planning* pamphlet, is part of a larger Policy Memorandum published in U.S.A. by the Center of International Studies at Princeton.

sian optimum. Be that as it may, all parties were agreed that something must be done about deflections.

To deal with them the suggestion was put forward that only products deemed to ' originate ' in the Area should be duty free and two criteria were envisaged for defining origin. (1) Under the percentage rule a product was deemed to originate in the Area if the percentage of the value of ' materials ' of non-Area origin were less than a given percentage of the final value of the product. (2) Specified processes would confer Area origin on the resulting products.

Both systems raised technical problems of their own: moreover if an attempt were made under either to guarantee that no deflections would occur, the effect would be to narrow very seriously the range of products which might hope to qualify for Free Trade Area treatment.

As a way out of these difficulties the Italian Minister for Foreign Trade, Signor Carli, proposed that goods should be allowed to move freely within the Area provided that the external tariffs applied by countries to these goods were within a margin on either side of a norm. If countries levied a tariff outside this margin, a compensating charge would be levied on all products traded between two countries in which the external tariffs were not sufficiently harmonized. Once again this solution raised technical difficulties. It was feared that the tendency to induce harmonization of tariffs might be achieved through a general raising of tariffs and in addition it might involve levying duties on products which were in fact entirely of Area origin. The attempts to eliminate distortions of one kind would be achieved by introducing distortions of another, albeit on a smaller scale.

Ultimately in the summer of 1958 it was agreed that none of the global solutions of the deflection problem could meet all cases satisfactorily and that separate studies should be undertaken for each ' sector ' in which any country foresaw difficulties, with a view to making particular arrangements for tariff reduction in each sector. This was a major concession by the British to the French who had adumbrated this line of attack at the beginning of the year. The French argument was not merely that the scale, and implicitly the dangers, of deflection might vary between sectors, but that the arrangements to reduce tariffs should be accompanied by the creation of conditions which would soften their consequences. There was a risk that any ultimate agreement along these lines might have been exceedingly cumbrous and so hedged about with compensatory devices to offset tariff differences, Commonwealth preferences and other sources of ' distortion ' as to leave very little room for an increased flow of trade.[1] Not infrequently in negotiations the desire to reach agreement for agreement's sake becomes more important than the consequences of any agreement: it looks as though this point was reached in mid-1958.

[1] No doubt the risk would be reduced if conditions of general economic expansion could be assured.

It is worth while, however, to dwell a little on the French insistence on the sector approach, for it represented in an extreme form the difference in approach to the questions at issue. For the French and, though perhaps to a lesser degree, the other members of the Six the Economic Community was not simply a device to liberalise trade among themselves. Trade liberalisation was only one part of a much broader plan. The consequence of liberalisation alone might be that some economies, or sectors of economies, would lose and others gain: but this was compensated by other aspects of the Community. This was certainly so for the French: their industrialists have never been enthusiastic about losing protection, but on the other hand the lion's share of the Overseas Investment Fund is destined for French territories. The Community was therefore a package deal. The point was made less bluntly but no less firmly by Professor Hallstein, president of the Commission of E.E.C., in a speech to the Parliamentary Assembly in March 1958 when he remarked that ' in view of the intimate connexion between all State measures in economic matters, the elimination of tariffs cannot lead to economically reasonable results or be maintained in the long run unless it is supplemented by a series of economico-political measures '. It was this same notion of the complementary character of the various elements in any agreement which made the French so hostile to the idea that associate members of the Area could retain freedom to vary tariffs with the outside world. They conceived any initial agreement as being a balance of gains and losses, and any such variation would be a unilateral disturbance of the balance. The British were prepared to concede the theoretical point, and to agree that a ' code of good conduct ' might be set up and also a complaints procedure to consider cases where a member claimed to have been injured by the tariff changes of another. They could not, however, agree that such changes could only be made after securing agreement of all the associate members of the Area.

The charge that the Community was ' discriminatory ' was also rebutted by the Six by an appeal to the package deal character of the Rome Treaty, of which harmonization, co-ordination of economic policies and so forth were the other elements. The Six claimed that the Community could only be regarded as discriminatory if they refused entry to other countries, and here the Treaty, formally at any rate, embodies the principle of the open door.

Underdeveloped countries

Five countries in O.E.E.C. can be characterised as under-developed in relation to the others: Eire, Turkey, Greece, Portugal and Iceland. There is little doubt that any agreement among all O.E.E.C. members would have to grant special treatment to them. In the early stages of negotiations in 1957 a special Working Party made some progress in

working out the character of this special treatment. Not unnaturally
these countries sought to delay the reduction of their own tariffs on industrial goods, which they considered necessary as part of their own pro-
grammes of industrial development: they placed emphasis on the freeing
of markets in the other members for their own agricultural produce: and
they called for the creation of European institutions to increase the supply
of capital for development.

Agriculture

Britain had originally proposed the complete exclusion of agricultural
products from any Free Trade Area measures. This position could not
be held against the arguments of important agricultural countries such as
Denmark that to deal only with industrial goods would be very unfair
to them. The Danes, indeed, were the only country to ask for ' free trade '
in agricultural products. All the other countries agreed that agriculture
needed ' special ' treatment, which, incidentally, is also accorded within
the Community, and it seems likely that had agreement seemed likely
on the major question of industrial goods, a parallel agreement on agriculture would have been possible.

Convertibility and the end of E.P.U.

With the excitements of the last stages of the O.E.E.C. negotiations,
and in particular the attempt to secure some multilateral agreement
about interim arrangements on January 1st, 1959, when the Rome Treaty
reductions came into force, we need not concern ourselves. The immediate
effects of the Economic Community reductions are not likely to do any
serious damage to non-members. In any case these excitements were
overshadowed by certain other events which must be recorded before we
try to sum up.

In October 1958 the I.M.F. agreed to recommend to its members a
50 per cent increase in quotas. This proposal had been put forward by
Britain, and in the months following there was a growing feeling that
sterling convertibility was imminent. The announcement of convertibility
was made in December 1958. It was accompanied by a similar move by the
leading European countries. France accompanied the restoration of
convertibility with a devaluation of the franc. She also announced her
decision to liberalise once more her O.E.E.C. trade to the ninety per
cent level. This last decision removed what had been one of the most
persistent irritants in the later stages of the Free Trade Area negotiations.
In June 1957 France had reimposed O.E.E.C. quotas for balance of payments reasons. She was committed to re-liberalise up to 60 per cent in
June 1958 and to 75 per cent in December 1958. She had felt unable to
fulfil the June 1958 commitment and other countries had felt that to have
given priority to the Rome Treaty reductions over the O.E.E.C. liberalisa-

tion would be violating the O.E.E.C. code of liberalisation. The decision to go to 90 per cent, a figure already reached by most of the major O.E.E.C. countries, was welcomed both for its effect in sweetening the political atmosphere and in reducing the ' discrimination ' implicit in the first stage of the Rome Treaty reductions.

The alternatives for Britain

The original British proposals for a Free Trade Area had the merit of being simple and practical. Negotiations could be limited to establishing rules about tariff and quota reductions to match those of the Community. They appeared to escape involvement in both complex administrative machinery and in the vague notion of harmonization. Nevertheless the British were driven step by step into these deeper waters. Their reluctance is understandable, and up to a point praiseworthy.

On the other hand the Six, with their emphasis on harmonization and the accompaniment of trade liberalisation by ' a series of economico-political measures ', also had an important point, and one cannot avoid the impression that the British reluctance was itself exaggerated by a doctrinaire adherence to free trade as such. In a revealing speech made as late as November 1958 Sir Edgar Cohen, Second Secretary of the Board of Trade, said:

' In a Free Trade Area, because each member is free to reduce his external tariff as he pleases *and* goods move freely between them, the lowest duties set the pace for the rest and the group tends to look outward and trade liberally. A customs union, on the other hand, is an economic unit and may, as such, pursue liberal or protectionist policies as its members may think fit.'[1]

If this is a true picture of the British attitude the ' intransigeance ' of the French becomes more understandable. One cannot predict with any great confidence whether trade liberalisation *as such* will bring widespread benefits. In a world in which all major economies are expanding fast, it can supplement the gains of higher productivity derived from technical progress with the further gains of international specialisation and competition, and while balance of payments disequilibria might still appear, their correction should not prove intractable. But if the major economies are sluggish, or if persistent creditor countries fail to make the necessary internal adjustments to eliminate chronic surpluses, free trade may only succeed in making things worse all round through spreading deflation.

Whether, if the British had seized this point and had placed greater emphasis on the need for institutions and the co-ordination of policies of *expansion*, it would have been possible to bring the negotiations of 1956–8 to a successful conclusion is an open question. Certainly there were other

[1] Speech to Institute of Public Administration, reported in *Board of Trade Journal*, 7th November, 1958.

political elements in the situation, e.g. Suez, which tended to separate Britain from France. Be that as it may it is hoped that in future negotiations the British delegations will stress the importance of policies of expansion and of prevention of balance of payments disequilibria.

No doubt the various private discussions which have been proceeding since the beginning of 1959 will show soon whether there is any point in trying to take up the original negotiations where they left off, and if not, what new kinds of approach are possible.

Should Britain, for example, attempt to seek more or less complete membership of the Community with, presumably, a good part of the Commonwealth associated in some form?

Should Britain join forces with other members of O.E.E.C. (or at any rate those with developed economies) in order (*a*) to ensure the largest bargaining strength for negotiation with the Six, or (*b*) to create a little free trade area of the ' outer seven ' of Britain, the Scandinavian countries, Austria, Portugal and Switzerland?

Or should we have recourse to bilateral negotiations with single members of the Six, or with the Community as a whole, bearing in mind that the British market itself is a large one for European products? Inevitably new approaches will have been announced by the time these words are published. But a further consideration of the more general principles and aims of policy is not out of place in the light of the new developments since the end of 1956.

THE GAINS FROM FREER TRADE WITH EUROPE: AN ESTIMATE

by HARRY G. JOHNSON

Aside from possible effects in stimulating competition and the spirit of enterprise, which are difficult to define, let alone measure, the main gains to be expected from freer trade between the United Kingdom and other European countries are those arising from its effects in increasing the income-producing efficiency of the country's resources. Such increases may accrue in three ways: through economies of scale in production made possible by enlargement of the market; through economies of specialization and division of labour resulting from freer trade; and through better terms of trade with the outside world. Of these, the first is unlikely to be very important for this country given the size of the market to which British industry already has access, and is in any case difficult to quantify. The third is unlikely to be significant for a Free Trade Area confined to manufactures, since Britain's dependence on imported food and materials would not be much reduced and a small reduction in her exports of manufactures to non-member countries would not have much effect in permitting higher prices. The substantial source of gain for the United Kingdom is therefore likely to be in the second direction, specialization and division of labour.

A rough idea of the magnitude of the gain from participation (or loss from non-participation) in the Common Market due to this cause can be derived from figures contained in the Economist Intelligence Unit's study *Britain and Europe*.[1] This volume gives estimates of the values of trade between this country and Europe in 1970 in the presence and the absence of a Free Trade Area, for eight major industries. These industries produced 55 per cent of the net value of British manufacturing output in 1950. In addition, estimates of trade quantities are given for another five major manufactured products, accounting for something under 18.5 per cent of net value of manufacturing output in 1950; these quantities can be translated into trade values by assuming an appropriate unit value, though the result is obviously less satisfactory than the figures for the other eight industries.[2]   Together, these thirteen industries accounted for about 50 per cent of U.K. exports to, and 25 per cent of imports from, the Continent in 1955.

From the estimates of trade values in 1970 on the two alternative assumptions, the effects of the Free Trade Area in increasing trade with Europe above what it would be if only the Common Market is established, can be estimated (*see Table 1 column 4, and Table 2 column 2*).[3]   The increase in the values of trade with the continent so derived do not, however, measure the gains that would result from the Free Trade Area, since exports use resources which could be devoted to other purposes, and imports must be paid for by exports. To obtain such measurements, it is necessary to begin by defining more precisely the nature of the economies of specialization permitted by freer trade.

On the export side, the gain arises from the opportunity to sell the products of the country's resources on better terms than would be possible otherwise, and could be measured by the loss of income that would result if the productive factors employed in meeting the additional demand created by the Free Trade Area had to be diverted to producing for the domestic or other foreign markets. Unfortunately this loss is not estimable

[1] The Economist Intelligence Unit Limited, *Britain and Europe*, London, 1957.

[2] The Unit values used below were derived as rough approximations from data contained in the industry chapters of *Britain and Europe*; they are stated in notes to the Tables, for the convenience of readers interested in re-calculating the estimates on other assumptions.

[3] The figures are not altogether satisfactory for the present purpose, since they include the effect of the assumption made by the Economist Intelligence Unit that the Free Trade Area will mean a greater increase (45 per cent as against 41 per cent) in G.N.P. by 1970 than would otherwise occur. This tends to make the following calculations produce an over-estimate of the gain from Free Trade.

TABLE 1

Estimated Maximum Gain on Exports from F.T.A.

Industry	Assumed C.M. Tariff Rate (%)	Total Exports to F.T.A. 1970		Additional Exports under F.T.A. as Against C.M., 1970	
		Value £(m)	Maximum Loss Estimate (£m)	Value (£m)	Maximum Loss Estimate (£m)
Iron and Steel	10	70	6.4	25	1.1
Non-ferrous Metals ...	10	40	3.6	15	0.7
Metal manufactures ...	17½	38	5.7	27	2.0
General engineering ...	17½	280	41.7	120	8.9
Electrical engineering ...	17½	225	33.5	132	9.8
Chemicals	17½	125	18.6	88	6.6
Hosiery	20	20	3.3	15	1.2
Clothing	20	24	4.0	20	1.7
Passenger cars ...	30	187	43.2	149	17.2
Commercial vehicles ...	30	70	16.1	58	6.7
Cotton fabrics	17	17	2.5	13	0.9
Wool fabrics	17	50	7.2	31	2.3
Man-made fibre fabrics	20	38	6.3	34	2.8
Totals		1,184	192.1	727	61.9

Assumed unit values: passenger and commercial vehicles £600;
cotton fabrics 12s. per lb; wool fabrics 25s. per lb;
man-made fibre fabrics 15s. per yd.

on the available information—it is arguable that it would not be great, since manufactures are fairly close substitutes on world markets. But it is possible to fix a maximum for the loss, since at the very worst the prices of the products concerned could be lowered enough to overcome the disadvantage of the Common Market tariff and permit their disposal in Europe.

This consideration actually leads to two estimates, according to what is assumed about the nature of the market and the price reductions necessary to offset the tariff. If the prices of all exports to Europe had to be reduced to the same extent, the maximum-loss estimate would be the value of exports to Europe under a Free Trade Area, multiplied by the proportion in the final price of the Common Market tariff rate which had to be offset.[1] This estimate, however, would be unrealistically large, since prices of some products, or to some markets, could be maintained while others were lowered. At the opposite extreme, price reductions might be confined to the minimum necessary to promote the particular transactions which would not take place in the absence of a Free Trade Area. In this case, the maximum-loss estimate would be (approximately) the value of the difference in exports to Europe due to the Free Trade Area, multiplied by half the proportion of the relevant tariff rate in the final price (since the price reductions required would have to offset the full weight of the tariff only in

[1] This proportion is related to the tariff rate by the formula $p = t/1 + t$, where p is the proportion and $100t\%$ is the *ad valorem* rate of duty on imports.

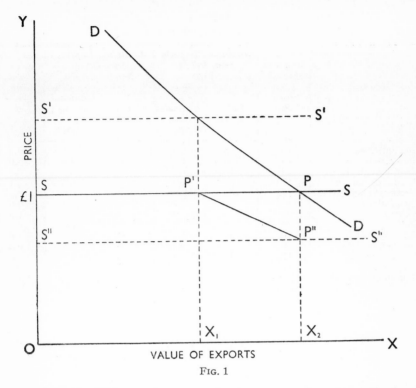

FIG. 1

extreme cases). Either estimate requires an assumption about the level of the Common Market tariffs, which in most cases can only be a reasoned approximation. The rates assumed,[1] and the two alternative estimates to which they lead, are presented in Table 1. On the first assumption, the maximum possible total loss on the industries represented would be of the order of £192 millions per year, while on the second, it would be only of the order of £62 millions per year. It should be stressed that these are maximum estimates, which assume that the goods concerned are useless outside the Continental market.

The theory underlying this calculation can be illustrated by reference to Figure 1. In the Figure, SS is the export supply curve of the products of a particular industry, measured in pounds' worth of domestic resources; DD is the European demand curve. With a tariff of SS' the quantity exported is OX_1, with free trade it is OX_2. What has to be done to export OX_2 in spite of the tariff depends on the nature of the industry's products. If these are perfect substitutes, the prices of all will have to be reduced until the new price plus the tariff is equal to OS: the supply curve becomes $S''S''$ and the loss incurred in selling OX_2 is $SS''P''P = SOX_2P \cdot SS''/OS$, i.e. the total value of free trade exports multiplied by the proportion of the

[1] Rough averages based on data in *Britain and Europe*.

D

TABLE 2

Estimated Gain on Imports from F.T.A.

Industry	Assumed British Tariff Rate (%)	Additional Imports from F.T.A. 1970		Additional Imports from Other Countries, 1970		Total Gain or Loss
		Value (£m)	Estimated Gain (m)	Value (£m)	Estimated Gain (+) or Loss (−) (£m)	
Iron and Steel ...	10	35	1.8	−21	−2.1	−0.3
Non-ferrous metals ...	15	20	1.5	+30	+4.5	+6.0
Metal manufactures ...	20	12	1.2	− 2	−0.4	+0.8
General engineering ...	17½	22	1.9	+ 3	+0.5	+2.4
Electrical engineering	17½	100	8.8	0	0.0	+8.8
Chemicals	17½	24	2.1	−12	−2.1	0.0
Hosiery	20	9	.9	+ 2	+0.4	+1.3
Clothing	20	7	.7	+ 1	+0.2	+0.9
Passenger cars ...	30	32	4.8	0	0.0	+4.8
Commercial vehicles ...	30	1	0.2	0	0.0	+0.2
Cotton fabrics ...	17½	10	0.9	+ 6	+1.0	+1.8
Wool fabrics	17½	5	0.5	+ 1	+0.2	+0.7
Man-made fibre fabrics	22½+11d. per lb	12	2.5	+ 3	+1.3	+3.8
Totals		290	27.7	+11	+3.5	+31.2

Assumed unit values: passenger and commercial vehicles £600; cotton fabrics 10s. per lb from F.T.A., 5s. per lb from rest; wool fabrics 15s. per lb; man-made fibre fabrics 3s. per yd. and 5 oz. per yd.

tariff in the final price. If the demand for each successive pound's worth of output is separate and independent, either because discrimination between buyers is possible or because the products are distinct, only the prices of the marginal exports will have to be reduced: the supply curve becomes $SP'P''$ and the loss incurred is $P'PP''$, which is approximately equal to $\frac{1}{2}P'P \cdot SS'' = \frac{1}{2}P'X_1X_2P \cdot SS''/OS$, i.e. half the value of the increase in exports under free trade, multiplied by the proportion of the tariff in the final price.

On the import side, the gain from freer trade arises from the opportunity provided to consume imported goods in place of more expensive domestic-ally-produced goods to which the purchaser has previously been directed by the tariff. This gain can be measured by the additional tariff revenue the Government could have collected if it had reduced the tariff on each individual item of the additional imports resulting from Free Trade just sufficiently to induce the purchaser to buy it (whether the tariff reduction is assumed to apply to the previous volume of imports doesn't matter, since this merely affects the distribution of income between purchasers of goods and the Government). It will be approximately equal to the change in the value of imports from the Free Trade Area, multiplied by half the tariff rate previously levied. Estimates of the gains from this source based

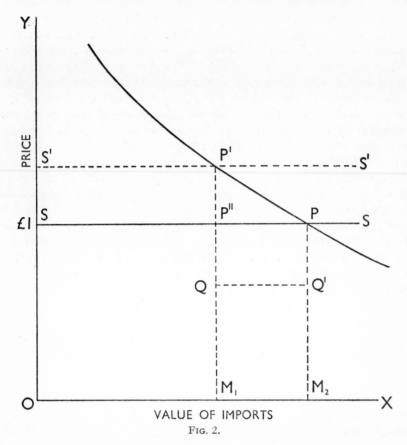

FIG. 2.

on the E.I.U. figures and assumed tariff rates are presented in the left half of Table 2; the total is of the order of £28 millions per year.

In addition to the gains from greater imports from Europe, however, it is necessary to take into account the fact that elimination of tariffs on trade with Europe will affect the value of trade with the rest of the world and so alter the amount of tariff revenue collected on that trade. Estimates of the difference that a Free Trade Area as against a Common Market only would make to British imports from outside Europe can be derived from the E.I.U. study and are presented in the right half of Table 2, together with the value of the difference on the assumed tariff rates. The resulting figure, a gain of £3.5 million per year, is admittedly rather suspect, and is largely attributable to the study's assumption that Gross National Product will be higher in 1970 with a Free Trade Area than without one.

The theory underlying the calculation on the import side is illustrated in Figure 2, where SS is the European supply curve of imports, measured in pounds' worth, $S'S'$ is that supply curve including the British tariff, and DD is the British demand curve. Elimination of the tariff increases imports from Europe from OM_1 to OM_2, resulting in a transfer from tariff revenue to consumers' surplus of $SS'P'P''$ and an increase in consumers' surplus (which could have been captured by discriminatory lowering of tariffs on marginal imports) of $P'P''P$, approximately equal to $\frac{1}{2}P'P'' \cdot P''P = \frac{1}{2}P''M_1M_2P \cdot S'S/OS$, i.e. half the value of the increase in imports multiplied by the tariff rate. To finance the extra imports, however, expenditure elsewhere has to be reduced by $P''M_1M_2P$, of which some part, say $P''QQ'P$, represents a reduction in government tax revenue. If it is expenditure on home-produced goods which is reduced, the re-absorption of the QM_1M_2Q' worth of resources in export production will generate new tax revenue which may be expected to replace the loss; but if it is expenditure on imports from non-European sources which is reduced, the loss of tariff revenue is not made good and must be deducted from the increase in consumers' surplus. Conversely, if imports from non-European countries are complementary with imports from (or exports to) Europe and so increase, the country benefits from the associated increase in tariff revenue. The loss (gain) is measured by the increase (decrease) in the value of imports, multiplied by the applicable tariff rate.

Putting the two sides of the picture together, we arrive at a maximum possible gain on the export side of £62–192 millions per year, and a gain on the import side of £31 millions a year, for the industries represented. These figures suggest orders of magnitude for the economy as a whole of, say, £125–£400 millions as the maximum gain on the export side, and £100 millions as the gain on the import side (bearing in mind that these industries are more important in exports than in imports). If the minimum figure for the maximum export gain is taken as a (probably excessive) approximation to the likely gain on that side, this would imply a total gain of the order of £225 millions—a difference of about 1 per cent on what the Economist Intelligence Unit estimates the Gross National Product is likely to be in 1970. This figure is very rough—more of a ' guesstimate ' than an estimate—but because of the way it is arrived at the order of magnitude is unlikely to be altered much by quite substantial changes in the assumed unit values or tariff rates on which it is based.

THE CASE FOR BRITISH ENTRY INTO THE EUROPEAN ECONOMIC COMMUNITY

By A. C. L. Day

In its fundamentals, the case for a British initiative to enter the Common Market must rest on political judgments. This does not mean, however, that the economist has nothing useful to say, nor even that he should merely regard himself as a technical adviser to the politicians. Although the decision and the foundations of the decision are predominantly political, so that purely economic arguments cannot clinch the case one way or the other, the political and economic elements in the case are so interrelated that the economist has much more than a mere technical expertise to offer. He is in a remarkably good position, compared with most other people, to argue the pros and cons of the case.

All of this was, in fact, equally true of the argument for the European Free Trade Area, and is true of the discussion of a more limited Free Trade Area between some of the countries outside the Common Market. The arguments for a European Free Trade Area, and a reason for hoping that the negotiations for a more limited Free Trade Area are based on fewer fundamental diplomatic ineptitudes on the part of the United Kingdom than the earlier abortive negotiations, rest largely on the political disadvantages of an economic split within Western Europe. In turn, the arguments for a Free Trade Area rested on a realisation of the limited validity of economic nationalism in a world where the small or medium-sized nation state is not a viable independent unit—a world in which so many things have to be done on a big scale if they are to be done at all, that a nation the size of Britain, let alone one the size of Italy, cannot aspire any longer to full Great Power status.

This realisation of the limits of economic nationalism has taken different forms in continental Europe from that in Britain. In Europe, emphasis has tended to be placed on the virtue of co-ordination and integration of the policies of different nations, with the aid of an elaborate structure of institutions of a type which always makes the British mind rather suspicious. In Britain, where the war left no memory of defeat and foreign invaders, and where the idea of the Commonwealth has always been available to help compensate for our post-war awareness of our reduced position in the world, the main force of the reaction to our realisation of the limits of economic nationalism has been directed, in the last few years, towards trying to achieve the advantages of a liberal trading world, based on the principles of comparative cost.

Nevertheless, there is the important common feature between British and continental attitudes, that there has been a reaction against economic nationalism—even if the differing forms which the reactions took go a long way towards explaining the failure of the Free Trade area negotiations in 1958. And the common feature is particularly apparent in the realisation mentioned a little earlier, that countries the size of Britain can no longer claim full Great Power status. This political judgment, based on economic and strategic factors, is fundamental to the whole of the rest of the argument of this paper. In addition, a fundamental assumption is that a period of relative decline in political power often induces an extremely wasteful megalomania, an excessive liking for prestige expenditure, and a temptation to try to live on past glories—all understandable enough, but likely to be extremely dangerous economically by inhibiting economic growth in the directions where it can most successfully be achieved.

There is evidence of these dangers in present-day Britain; but they are by no means overwhelming, and one of the great virtues of close relationships with a closely-knit group of countries such as the Common Market, is that by throwing ourselves into a large and successful political and economic bloc, Britain will be able to retain a political power and influence that will be impossible if she is forced into the position of a Japan, lying, rather isolated, off the shores of Europe. The argument is one of retaining power by co-operating with a group of reasonably like-minded countries.

This same argument could also be adduced, though rather less strongly, for the European Free Trade Area project; as will be argued at length shortly, that project must have involved a very high degree of integration of policies, both economic and more broadly political, if it were to be successful. And all the other closely-related arguments for a Free Trade Area—such as the virtues of trade creation in a world where different countries have different comparative advantages, the narrower benefits of trade diversion from outsiders, and the intangible but very powerful argument that businessmen try harder under a spur of competition—all these arguments apply at best equally strongly to the question of Common Market membership.

Beyond the fact that Common Market membership would give Britain a greater say in the political counsels of Europe than mere membership of a looser Free Trade Area, the ultimate argument for negotiating Common Market membership rather than a Free Trade Area depends on a belief that the one is more likely to be negotiable than the other. Most of the rest of this paper will be concerned with analysing the implications of this statement. These implications, and the questions they raise, can be grouped into three sets: a belief that the original Free Trade Area concept is dead, a belief that the economic advantages to Britain of Common Market membership are at least as great as those of membership of a European Free Trade Area while the disadvantages and difficulties have often been overstated, and thirdly on a belief that there is a fair chance that a British initiative for full membership could be made acceptable and indeed welcome to the Europeans.

The first question is that of whether some kind of Free Trade Area covering the whole of Europe can still be negotiated. That is the declared ultimate aim of the British Government and of the other members of the Outer Seven (namely the Scandinavian countries, Austria, Portugal and Switzerland), in trying to establish a narrower Free Trade Area between themselves. It is impossible to predict whether or not they will ultimately succeed; but the auguries are not too favourable, and there is a real danger that the next few years will see an increasing economic split within western Europe. The auguries are rather unfavourable, because the Outer Seven proposals only put strong pressure on the groups within the Six (such as German industrialists and the Benelux governments) which have always been strong supporters of an all-European Free Trade Area. Remarkably little pressure is put on the other hand, on French industrialists, who are not greatly concerned with the markets of the Seven, or on nationalist groups in France who would in any case like to keep Britain out of continental Europe.

Lying behind these doubts about hopes of re-opening the door that was slammed shut in December 1958, is a basic and simple truth about the European Economic Community that is still not sufficiently realised, namely, that it is a serious attempt to establish a European Community, both economic and ultimately political. The attempt may still fail—but its real strength has never been properly understood in Whitehall. If one is setting up an economic community, inevitably there must be some discrimination by members in favour of one another and therefore some discrimination against outsiders, just as the Benelux customs union involved some discrimination against outsiders; and inevitably outsiders cannot reasonably expect to be allowed into the club on their own terms. There has always been a clash of basic conception between the ideas of the Six, based on twentieth century ideas of conscious economic integration and the ideas of Whitehall, based on an idealised version of nineteenth century free trade and national sovereignty.

Beyond the purely economic points, there lies the ultimate fact that the aim of the Rome Treaty is to establish a high degree of political integration in Europe. Reasonably enough, the view is held in the Six that the countries which are not willing to accept this political involvement cannot expect to be able to demand the benefits of membership of the Community: whether their unwillingness is for reasons of neutrality, as with the Swiss and Swedes, or because they think, as many people in Britain seem to do, that such involvement would reduce our political power. And it is important to notice that something like this analysis of the situation would be shared even by the many continental supporters of the European Economic Community who would like to have seen the other European countries associated with the Community through the establishment of some sort of Free Trade Area. When it came to the point, none of the Six was willing to risk wrecking the Community for the sake of a wider but much weaker grouping.

Of course it is quite impossible to predict the precise nature of both the political and the economic integration that will come about as a result of the progressive development of the Community. The nationalistic Government of de Gaulle in France is obviously a powerful force, for the time being at any rate, which is operating to reduce the power of the integrationist elements in the Rome Treaty. At the same time, the de Gaulle—Adenauer foreign policies are doing a great deal to establish the idea of the Six as a closely-knit political bloc—albeit a bloc of more independent states than would be liked by the ' Europeans ' such as Monnet who were co-responsible for the signing and ratification of the Rome Treaty.

Since it will take something like fifteen years for the Community to come into full operation, there is still plenty of room for doubt about how tightly integrated the economic policies of its members will eventually be. The Rome Treaty itself is certainly quite sufficiently flexible to allow for a wide range of possibilities. This, indeed, is one of the powerful arguments for British membership; all that is clear is that some sort of bloc is being established; its precise nature will depend to a large extent on the policies of its members. A liberally-minded British Government could, by membership, give the Community a markedly liberal twist; a Socialist Government here could find plenty of room within the Treaty to encourage the sort of ends it considered desirable, not merely within narrow national boundaries but throughout the Community. One of the striking features of the British opposition to membership of the Community has been its defeatism: the belief that the Europeans would impose their policies on us and the failure to realize that we should be in a very strong position to persuade them to follow our predilections.

Although the Community will take some fifteen years to come fully into existence, many of its main features, such as the agricultural arrangements and the full details of the ultimate external tariff, will be determined long before then. Since Britain is deeply concerned with these matters, the case is strong for saying that if Britain is to enter the Community, it should do so soon, rather than waiting for some unpredictable propitious moment, when these matters will already have been determined, and when many of the other characteristics of the Community will be settling into some mould or other.

The really big question still remains to be answered, however. This is the second of the three outlined above, namely, whether the economic advantages to Britain in joining the European Community would outweigh the disadvantages. This can in turn be usefully considered in two parts;

the economic advantages and disadvantages of some close relationship with the Community, whether in a Free Trade Area or in full membership, and the economic advantages and disadvantages of full membership, compared with the situation of membership of a Free Trade Area of the type envisaged in the later stages of the negotiations in 1958.

It is unnecessary here to devote too much time to the first of these two parts of the question. A great deal has already been argued, at differing levels of sophistication, about the *pros* and *cons* of British participation in a European Free Trade Area, and there is no point in rehearsing them at length here, for the reason that the Free Trade Area idea did receive a remarkable degree of political acceptance in Britain, and still more remarkably, little effective opposition. British industry, and insofar as they had articulate ideas on the matter, the majority of the British electorate seems either to have actively wanted a Free Trade Area, or to have been willing to tolerate it. For the sake of the present argument, therefore, it is safe to accept this political judgment and to move on from it.

Of course, this is only a device to avoid working over old territory; the will of the electorate can hardly be equated with economic wisdom. All that I propose to say here about this old territory is that I believe this political judgment to have been based on a reasonable appraisal of the economic situation, in particular on a view that there are big potentialities for developing mutually advantageous trade between industrial economies which are, broadly speaking, competitive rather than complementary in their present trade.

More attention will have to be given to the really basic question, which is that of the advantages and disadvantages of full membership of the Community, compared with an all-European Free Trade Area.

One set of arguments here concerns the other European countries, outside the Six, who consider at this moment that they cannot join the Six. They can be divided into three categories; the neutrals, the Scandinavians and the peripheral underdeveloped countries.

The main ' Neutrals ' are Switzerland and Austria; by treaty or through historical policy, they are unable to accept full Community commitments. As an alternative to complete exclusion from European economic arrangements, they are willing to enter a Little Free Trade Area, mainly (it seems) in the hope of reaching an ultimate bargain with the Six. But, as we have seen, this is not really a particularly high hope; it is hard to avoid the conclusion that it would be better for the Swiss and the Austrians to negotiate to enter the customs union of a broader Community, including Britain, while not accepting the other obligations of membership of the Community. This solution would probably be acceptable to the Six because of the facts of geography and the awareness of the very special political positions of both of these countries. Certainly it has advantages for Austria and Switzerland, who must find it hard to forgo trade ties with the Six for the sake of links with Britain and Scandinavia; Austria sends over half her total exports to the Six and less than one-tenth to Switzerland, Britain and Scandinavia, while Switzerland sends nearly two-fifths of her total exports to the Six and only about 15 per cent to Britain, Scandinavia and Austria.

The trade links of Scandinavia with Britain are much stronger relatively to those with the Six than those between Britain on the one hand and Switzerland and Austria on the other. But even at the moment there are strong pressures in Scandinavia (notably Denmark and to a less extent Norway) for membership of the Community, for the sake of access to the food markets of the Six. Sweden is in a more equivocal position, and is allowing herself to take the lead in pushing for a Little Free Trade Area; she is less interested in food exports than the other Scandinavians, and is also politically neutral. But she could probably also negotiate some sort of special relationship with the Community, as in the cases of Switzerland and Austria.

This leaves the question of the peripheral countries—a question which only has to be posed for its triviality to become apparent. There was never much chance that these countries would be full working members of the Free Trade Area; if the rest of Europe joins or becomes closely associated with the Community, arrangements could undoubtedly be made with the peripheral countries if they seemed politically desirable.

We can now turn to the second set of arguments against British membership of the Community—the arguments that membership would involve Britain in unacceptable commitments. To consider this question means going back to fundamentals, and considering the reasons for Britain's unwillingness to enter the European Economic Community. In the early days of the Free Trade Area negotiations there seemed to be an almost limitless number of reasons why Britain could not adhere to the Rome Treaty. But as time passed, it became clear that many of these reasons were based on misconceptions of what was intended by the Six. The greatest misunderstanding concerned agriculture; the British and continental positions moved much nearer together when it was realized that there would not be free movement of agricultural goods within the Community, but merely a ' managed market '. In addition, there were quite a number of similar but less publicised misconceptions which were slowly straightened out in the course of the negotiations, so that by the summer of 1958 Britain was willing to adhere to rules that in most respects were very much the same as those accepted by the Six. For example, a great bugbear was made at one time of proposals for allowance for ' harmonisation ' of social charges. In fact, however, careful investigation showed that the amount of money involved was quite small anyway (an informed guess was that it would mean 2s. 6d. one way or the other on a ton of coal —a very labour-intensive commodity) and that a reasonable degree of harmonisation was quite acceptable to Britain in a Free Trade Area. Again, by the summer, Britain was more than willing to accept some sort of majority voting principle on the larger policy questions. The O.E.E.C. type of unanimity rule was seen not to be enough for the Free Trade Area, any more than for the Common Market; it came to be realised by the British that there must be some system of majority weighted voting. In fact, one of the main differences between the British and the French has been the unwillingness of the French to have majority voting in the Free Trade Area, because of their dislike of the whole conception.

In effect, therefore, the type of Free Trade Area that would have been acceptable to Britain would have involved us in a very close degree of integration of economic policies with those of continental Europe. A Free Trade Area, in spite of its name, could never have simply operated a nineteenth-century *laissez-faire* system; inevitably it would have involved us in extremely close co-operation with Europe in matters of economic policy. And just like the European Economic Community, the Free Trade Area would have been at the same time a restrictive and an expansionary grouping—restrictive because it excludes outsiders, and expansionary because it increases freedom within the group of countries making it up. In all these respects, Britain was willing to enter into precisely the same kinds of relationship as are already being established within the Community.

Nor was this willingness to enter into significant commitments which extended beyond a simple expansion of trade by any means limited to economic questions. It is realised by the majority of far- sighted politicians (including the Prime Minister himself) that Britain's political future lies with Europe—and a major aim of the Free Trade Area was to encourage a movement towards this political integration. But the question still remains, whether it would be acceptable to the British voter to take on the political commitments involved in the tighter political integration implicit in the European Economic Community. This is, indeed, a difficult question to answer; but it is at least worthy of note that British political opposition to the Free Trade Area was much less than most people expected and this may very well imply a public willingness to become involved politically in Europe which is much greater than most people had thought. At least it would be enlightening to know what would be the reaction to a real and imaginative political lead. Plenty of people realize the implications of isolation on a small island that will soon not even be large enough to be a satisfactory aircraft carrier.

Such a political lead would undoubtedly have to pay attention to the powerful emotional ties to the Commonwealth—it would have to be presented as a move to bring the Commonwealth and Europe closer together; perhaps even to make Europe a sort of associate member of the Commonwealth. It is at this point, of the Commonwealth link, that the argument works back again to economics. It was on the question of the external tariff that negotiations for a Free Trade Area broke down. Apart from the question of the Commonwealth tariff, there are two other reasons why Britain has felt unable to consider a common tariff policy with the Community, either within a customs union or by a degree of tariff integration envisaged in the Carli Plan. It will be useful to consider these two subsidiary reasons first, before considering the major problem of the Commonwealth Preference System, by which we give tariff preferences to Commonwealth countries and receive preferences from many Commonwealth countries in return.

One subsidiary argument against accepting the common tariff of the Six, is that it would raise our industrial costs by imposing tariffs on raw materials. In fact this argument is trivial, as far as the country as a whole is concerned, although manufacturers in some industries would be adversely affected. Only a very few of the important materials would be affected—notably some non-ferrous metals and timber; on the basis of estimates of likely tariffs, our total industrial costs would rise by well under 1 per cent over a ten to fifteen-year period.

The second subsidiary argument is that Britain is helping the underdeveloped countries by maintaining tariff-free entry for the manufactures of Commonwealth countries such as Hong Kong and India. On the other hand, it is argued that the European countries are unwilling to follow such a liberal policy, which is likely to prove an increasingly important matter as the underdeveloped countries increase their production of the simpler manufactures. This is certainly an argument of substance. It does ignore two things, however. One is that Britain is less liberal than some European countries to the major non-Commonwealth supplier of manufactures among the poorer countries, namely, Japan. The other is that British pressure within the Community could lead to a rather more liberal policy for the whole group.

The really important argument, however, is that Britain cannot afford to abandon the present Commonwealth Preference system. The important point about Commonwealth Preference, however, is that it is steadily disappearing, as a result of dissatisfaction with its working in the other Commonwealth countries. Recent Australian and New Zealand reductions in preferences show the way the wind is blowing; and even the Canadian Government, with its protestations of interest in the Commonwealth link, is only willing to freeze a range of preferences. The preferences enjoyed by Britain are substantial—about 4–5 per cent on the value of our total exports to the Commonwealth; and of course some industries (such as motor cars) do much better. But there can be no doubt that Commonwealth Preference is an asset which will waste away steadily over the next ten or fifteen years. The danger for our industry is that this will happen, at the same time as we are being excluded from many European markets by the customs union of the Six.

Fortunately, there is a way out of this dilemma, which has been marked out for us by France, whose overseas territories (like those of Holland and Belgium) are in an ' external relationship ' with the Community. This means that the products of these territories will have free entry into the Six, while the manufactures of the Six will in turn have preferential entry into them, but subject to protection of the infant industries of those territories, by ' customs duties which correspond to the needs of their development and to the requirements of their industrialisation.'

A similar bargain for the Commonwealth countries would extend Commonwealth Preference to Europe, giving Europe the favours in Commonwealth markets enjoyed by British industry, in exchange for wider entry for Commonwealth foodstuffs and raw materials into Europe.

Whether such a bargain would be negotiable, would only be seen if it were seriously considered by the governments concerned; and so far there is no evidence that the British Government has taken the initiative to suggest such an idea. But it is on Britain that the burden of this task lies; otherwise individual Commonwealth countries (notably Australia and New Zealand) are likely to strike direct bargains with the Six. Certainly, there seems a strong case for these countries to consider giving the same tariff to European goods as to British, in return for guaranteed or increased European markets for their farm products. As for the other Commonwealth countries, apart from Canada, the general picture is one of giving remarkably little in the way of preferences to Britain, so that the bargain would be relatively unimportant anyway. Canada is undoubtedly the most awkward case, both because of the fear of seeming to discriminate against the United States, and because certain Canadian products, such as aluminium and wheat, might prove embarrassingly competitive with the products of the Six, if free entry were allowed into Europe. Perhaps the answer to the first problem would be to remove all dollar import restrictions, while the answer to the second would have to be some sort of special arrangements for a few of these critical commodities; what would in any case be part of an agricultural bargain, and quota restrictions might be placed on Canadian aluminium into continental Europe. Certainly, there is no reason to think that agreement is impossible.

At the same time arrangements of this sort would benefit European manufacturers, by giving them greater access to Commonwealth markets; and they would destroy the argument that Britain has been trying to get the best of both worlds. The effective objections would come from French colonial interests, which would suffer on coffee, cocoa and bananas; whether these objections would be overriding depends mainly on what continental attitudes would be to a British initiative to enter the Common Market on precisely the same terms as the present members. This question will be considered shortly.

Meantime, it is necessary to consider the effects on Britain of an extension of Commonwealth Preference to Europe.

Oddly enough, arrangements between the Commonwealth countries and Europe would not merely benefit Europe and the Commonwealth; Britain would gain as well. For one thing, this would be the sort of bargain which would make it worthwhile for Commonwealth countries to strive to maintain Commonwealth Preference instead of allowing it to erode. For another, such an arrangement would remove the only remaining economic barrier to British entry into the customs union of the European Economic Community—with all that means in terms of opportunities for our exports. And, in fact, it removes the only real remaining economic barrier to our full membership of the European Community; the only remaining Rome Treaty commitment which Britain has not been willing to accept in the Free Trade negotiations is that of free labour movement. Undoubtedly, there would be strong trade union opposition to any acceptance of the principle of freedom of labour movement from Europe to Britain. But if a Government could dare accept the principle, the trade unions would come to realize that there would not be a great flood of workers coming in. For one thing, labour is not very mobile; compared with the Six, Britain is distant and socially and linguistically unwelcoming to the Italians, who have the great labour surplus; and in any case, the trade unions will no doubt contrive to limit entry to many trades, even when foreign labour could come in easily. Closer investigation shows that this freedom would not amount to much as far as Britain is concerned.

The choice, then, that faces Britain is a real challenge to our imagination. Either we drift, and find ourselves excluded from free access to European markets, while coming to enjoy less and less in the way of favours in Commonwealth markets; or we make a great effort of imagination and will, and initiate the complicated bargaining process leading to our entry into the European Community, together with an external association for all the Commonwealth countries that desire it.

The final question to be considered is that of the likely European reaction to a British initiative of this kind. Undoubtedly, the auguries are less favourable than they were during the final months of the Free Trade Area negotiations, when the nationalism of the French Government was less powerful and effective than it is now. One has to admit that the time has passed when Britain could be sure of a wide-open welcome to membership of the Community—an admission which reflects the extent to which western Europe is already split. And it has to be admitted that even if Britain were willing to enter the Community, bargaining about voting rights would be complicated. But the fact remains that it would be incredibly difficult for the members of the Six to refuse to admit Britain if she wholeheartedly was willing to take on the obligations as well as the benefits of membership. At the very least, it would be a tragedy if in a few years time, we found we had once again missed a European bus, for want of trying.

THE NEED FOR EXPANSION

By R. F. HARROD

In my previous article I suggested that it should allay the fears of those who are alarmed by the rigours of competition in an open European Free Trade Area, to consider the problem in terms of a probable, or possible, expansion of European production. If in the next ten or fifteen years each country concentrated its *increase* of production on the lines in which it was best fitted by the principle of national specialization, this would produce a very great change in the industrial structure of each country and it might well happen that the reduction of output required by each country in the lines in which it was not favoured would be easily manageable. This happy conclusion implied an expanding production all round.

Since that time two things have happened. One is the temporary failure of the attempt to get a Free Trade Area covering all the O.E.E.C. countries. The other has been the recession, or pause, in the industrial production of most European countries.

Consolation is derived from the fact that there was no actual decline in overall industrial production in Europe in 1958. There was a decline in some countries and an abatement in the rate of progress of the countries taken as a collection. While a more precise chronological sub-division would be required to give a full and true picture, the following yearly figures may be of interest.

TABLE

	O.E.E.C. Countries	
	Average annual rates of increase 1952–1957	Rates of increase between 1957–1958
Index of industrial production	6.8%	1.5%
Imports from countries *other* than O.E.E.C. countries, the U.S.A. and Canada (value)	5.5%	−4.6%
Ditto adjusted by applying index of prices of imported foodstuffs and raw materials	5.6%	1.1%
Volume of all imports	8.4%	0
Volume of all U.S. imports	3.1%	2.7%

The slowing down in the rate of increase of production in 1957/8 compared with the preceding 5 years is clearly marked. Imports shown in the second line may give a rough indication of the trend of the imports of Europe from the countries mainly depending on primary products. Here the change-over is more marked, but the decline shown in 1958 is to be accounted for by the drop in primary product prices. The third line attempts to give a (very rough) adjustment for the decline in prices. The abatement in the rate of increase of imports is marked and corresponds fairly well with the abatement in the increase of industrial production. The welfare of primary producers depends naturally not only on the volume of their sales, but also on the value received. Their plans had been geared to the increasing demand of previous years, and, when that increase slowed down so notably, the balance of supply and demand was thrown out and the decline in the value of those products was the consequence. It is to be observed that the abatement in the rate of increase occurred fairly early in 1957 and would account for the decline of prices which began in the course of that year.

A line has been added showing the volume of U.S. imports. The annual increase in the 1952–1957 quinquennium is seen to be much less than that of Europe. In those years Europe was making a spurt of recovery from post-war dislocations; its increase was concentrated upon industrial production, whereas in the U.S. industrial production and other elements in the Gross Domestic Product rose more nearly in proportion. On the other hand the U.S. change-over in importation in 1958 was much smaller, one might almost say negligible. In 1957 there was no decline of American importation from any of the broad regions, except Canada. Thus, although the Americans, unlike Europe, had what may be called a slump in 1957–8, it was so short that it did not have a great effect on the outside world. There seems little doubt that the causes of the world-wide recession of 1958 lay in the European pause of 1957–8 rather than in the sharp, but short, American recession.

It is not to be expected that the steep rates of increase shown by Europe in the 1952–1957 quinquennium will be maintained, as they were due to special post-war circumstances. On the other hand it is not clear that in the period ahead the countries of Europe will again encompass rates of increase of output fully in line with their potential capacity. There may be anxieties and inhibitions. An interesting point is that the authorities in many of the countries of Europe pleaded, in relation to proposals for re-expansionist measures in 1958, that it would be dangerous to push on with them on the ground of their weakening exports. They feared that strong re-expansion, entailing possible substantial increases in their imports, might endanger their foreign exchange position and currency stability. But if these declines in exports are examined, it will be found that the major part of the declines was in the exports of European countries to each other. The primary producing countries appear, despite their declining incomes, to have maintained their imports better, by drawing on their reserves or obtaining loans and grants, etc. Thus each of the European countries was tending to hold back from expansion because the exports of each to other European countries were weak.

Surely this points very clearly to the need for greater co-operation between the European countries. This could be effectuated through a

quickening of the activities already undertaken by the O.E.E.C. group.
Such co-operation could be based upon the recognition by the governments
concerned that there would be advantage in the different countries of
Europe supporting each other in a policy of expansion and that Europe
had a special duty to the under-developed countries in maintaining their
increase of exports from those countries. As the panel of G.A.T.T.
experts, which reported in 1958, observed, the best way of all for mature
countries to help the less developed countries is to maintain a steady
increase in their purchases from them.

The more moderate increase in American imports may be brought back
to our attention in this connection. The basic reason for this is probably
not unconnected with the considerations that Professor Galbraith has
popularized. His contention may well be true that the U.S. is approaching
a point in which future expansion will be directed less to an ever-increasing
material output and more to ' services ', including those of education and
culture. Indeed a comparison of the increase of industrial production in
the U.S. and the increase in the Gross Domestic Product, suggests that the
trend foreseen by Professor Galbraith has already set in, although only to
a moderate extent. But what benefits the under-developed countries
directly is not the increase of education and culture in the mature countries, but their increase in material production leading to increased requirements for imports. Now the European countries still have a long way to
go in their requirements for production of a strictly material kind. Their
aggregate imports from outside Europe are now substantially larger than
those of the U.S. Thus the well-being of the under-developed countries
will depend much more on whether the European countries maintain
the expansion of production of which they are capable than on whether
the U.S. does.

It cannot be laid down in advance precisely what form co-operation
for expansion should take. Some might think it desirable to lay down a
' target ' rate, such as 3 per cent, or 4 per cent, a year. This may be too
rigid. But at least it could be a common thought that a steady rate of
expansion is the objective of all the countries. Within the machinery of
O.E.E.C., countries could exchange notes on their own successes and
failures. Each country should show what precisely it is doing to maintain
steady growth. Periodic reports could be issued, not only on achievement,
but also on the policies that each country was professing to follow to
improve the achievement. Then it would probably come out clearly
from time to time, as in 1958, that the anxieties inhibiting some countries
were due mainly to the laggardness of other European countries, itself
due to similar anxieties—that there was in fact a vicious circle.

This is not the place to enlarge upon the kind of measures required to
sustain growth, nor upon the obvious fact that simultaneous action by all
countries, for instance in the domain of Bank Rate and other forms of

E

monetary policy, would enable each to go forward more securely. Out of such consultations might arise something like a common European policy of expansion.

I would suggest that if thoughts such as these could be crystallized and instructions given to O.E.E.C. representatives right away, this would be a better next line of approach than an immediate renewal of negotiations on the Free Trade Area question. For out of a common policy to promote expansion would arise a common sense of purpose and solidarity of feeling. In the atmosphere thus created it would come to seem absurd to be inhibited from moving towards freedom of trade by the kind of technical difficulties that were so prominent in the recent discussions. Furthermore a joint policy of expansion would tend to remove the real anxieties that lay behind the emphasis that some countries placed on the technical difficulties. Let a joint policy of expansion be officially recognized now, and put into operation, and I feel confident that success in the Free Trade Area negotiations would follow in due course as a corollary.

UNEQUAL PARTNERS[1]

By T. Balogh

I. The Way to Nowhere

I have always disliked and distrusted the so-called Common Market concept of uniting Europe. I disliked it because I felt, and still feel, doubtful whether so negative a project of unifying such extremely disparate societies and economies, and their subjection to ' free competition ', to the law of the jungle, in their relations with one another can do anything but make the strong richer and the weak poorer. I also suspected that the social tensions which continue to exist domestically, despite the steady integration of society through the so-called Welfare State and despite the feeling of national solidarity, would in an international (though intra-European) context be magnified, give rise to feelings of rivalry, and thus undermine rather than strengthen the capacity of Europe to stand up to the Soviet challenge.

When I wrote my contribution to the *Symposium* in 1957 I still hoped that British bargaining power would be used either to oppose successfully

---

[1] This essay was written in the summer of 1959. Events since, and especially the formation of the Outer-Seven-EFTA, do not, in my opinion, necessitate any significant change. The Six have slightly relaxed their discrimination against outsiders but have refused to accept Britain as a partner: all concessions have been made on a ' most favoured nation ' basis. This invites American support and stultifies the British efforts.

(in G.A.T.T. or by influencing opinion within the Six) the coming into being of the Common Market scheme, or to modify it to such a degree as to make it a basis ' less risky and more hopeful for a full development of European productivity and productive power '. The second alternative was never pursued, and the first was not thought to be necessary. The British Government was misinformed about the likelihood of the Rome Treaties being first signed, and then ratified, unless opposed by Britain.[1] Mr. Worswick chides the ' Europeans ' for their ' strain of almost mystical fervour ' which, he says, is ' uncongenial to British statesmen, administrators and economists '. But the fervour of the Europeans is mainly political and they have up to the present been realists, in the sense that they carried their partners with them without much questioning as to the economic costs and advantages of the new political unit. The British, on the other hand, can be accused of a much less realistic attitude of mystical fervour, if not dogmatic frenzy, in the economic field where it is less easy to understand and impossible to condone.

As it happens, it was probably Colonel Nasser who was mainly responsible for the establishment of the Common Market. The most powerful resistance to the conception (just as its most energetic propagandists) had always been French: the protectionist antipathy of entrepreneurs was boosted by nationalist distrust. Without the isolation following the defeat of the Suez invasion the French parliament would not have voted for the ratification of the Rome Treaties. Even so, it was a narrow victory. In Italy it was only the middle-sized firms which were in opposition; the large firms were certain that they would be able to escape unfavourable consequences (if any—their wage costs were relatively low) by cartel arrangements. Italian labour supported the Common Market, because of the possibility of emigration to Germany lessening the problems of the depressed areas. Moreover, in Italy the nationalist spirit was entirely in favour of joining because, unlike the French, the Italians even on the extreme right could not hope to achieve world power except as members of a more embracing community. The German attitude was more ambivalent. Professor Erhard was quite willing to face a universalist solution and thought that the formation of a bloc might not yield as great an advantage to Germany as a completely open European system. His preference for ' free ' trade in Europe, in contrast to that of the British Board of Trade, was rational. Germany in the period between 1949 and 1958 had established itself as the unchallenged economic leader in Europe, and displaced England from the second place as manufacturing exporter and as a shipbuilder. German leadership in heavy industries, including chemicals and electricity, was also restored. Despite full employment, German productivity was increasing relentlessly while unit costs lagged behind, so that

---

[1] Just as in the subsequent period it was completely misinformed about the likely strength of the Franco-German *entente*, even after General de Gaulle's *coup d'état*.

full employment did not interfere with, but rather went parallel with and was maintained by huge export surpluses. Moreover German exports to Britain and the Little Seven were, if less, at any rate of the same order of magnitude as to the partners in the prospective Common Market, and she could fear, especially in Sweden and Austria, some displacement. These considerations were in the event overborne by Dr. Adenauer's determination to enlist Franco-Italian support for his international political policy.

It was one of the main blunders of British economic and political diplomacy that it did not realise the essential complementarity of the French need for economic and Adenauer's need for political support from one another. In the event the Rome Treaties were ratified, and renewed urgency was given to the renegotiation of the relationship between the new powerful central European unit and the other countries in O.E.E.C., including Britain. Carefully selected items relating to the negotiations have been published by the British Government.[1] Little emerges from these rather formal documents of the process of horse-trading that must have gone on, by which the Common Market countries, and especially France, first persuaded the British Government not to press its case against the Common Market in the G.A.T.T. to its logical conclusion, nor to declare its hostility or make conditions for joining.

Whatever might be said about the appropriateness of the Common Market as a solution to the problem of Europe (and I have given my reasons for distrust in my earlier contribution), these misgivings in no way support the British approach to the problem. If the Common Market approach contains insufficient safeguards,[2] the British Free Trade Area contained not only no safeguards but, being restricted to industrial goods, demanded unilateral concessions from the weaker countries of Europe while we hoped (being in an intermediate stage) to recoup ourselves for the losses to be suffered by a German invasion of our own markets by destroying the industries in the countries which are still weaker in the manufacturing field. It is now obvious that this attempt came to grief in the early stages, and by the autumn of 1958 the British Government had to make very decided concessions. In the end negotiations broke down on the question of common tariffs and the so-called harmonisation issue. I shall endeavour to show that in both cases the Board of Trade in its dogmatic frenzy was trying to safeguard Britain against imaginary perils while exposing British industry to fundamental dangers and a terrible threat.

[1] *Negotiations for a Free Trade Area*, Cmnd. 648, January 1959. Mr. Maudling paid me the compliment of trying to refute my charge, expressed in an article (*New Statesman*, February 7th, 1959) that the documents were selected. He confirmed what I had suspected: only items which had become part of his committee's documentation were published. It is of course the practice of these committees not to put anything into their documents except with the consent of all member governments.

[2] It must be admitted that its treatment of underdeveloped areas is far more enlightened than the British official attitude has ever been.

The imaginary dangers were the alleged effect of a common tariff on the cost of production in Britain. The real threat consists of exposure to a more dynamic economy having institutionally renounced the right of protecting oneself and without any compensating advantage of receiving organised help to achieve a greater equality of opportunity.[1]

It is easy to say now that such a threat by the U.S., exemplified by a chronic dollar shortage, never really existed and that the unequal increase in productivity was not an important issue. In point of fact it took the world eleven years and $62 billion of U.S. grants and government loans to recover at least temporarily from the dollar shortage, and even in 1958 the American Government was still making loans or grants of just under $2.8 billion abroad on top of military expenditure of $3.4 billion and military transfers of $2.5 billion. In addition private capital outflow amounted to $2.8 billion. Forsooth, this is not quite ' the high living and high spending ' through which Lord Keynes hoped to solve the problem in 1946.

Yet we have learned nothing from this lesson. The British objection to entry into the Common Market was mainly concerned with the threat that ' linking our price levels to those of France will have disastrous effects on our competitive position in export markets outside of Europe '.[2] The French objection to the British entry was that by obtaining supplies cheaper they would be able to compete devastatingly in their market without having to shoulder the other obligations of the Rome Treaties. Quite apart from the fact that the so-called Carli suggestion could have been adopted to equalise costs, the quantitative impact was grossly exaggerated. In the main, real conflict is restricted to very few commodities, of which aluminium, lead and zinc are the most important. Out of £754m. imports of raw materials from the Commonwealth, those falling into this category represented a trivial figure (£50m.) in 1956. There are no tariffs on the main raw materials in either Britain or the proposed Common Market.

[1] It is entirely characteristic of the futility of the comparative static approach that, e.g., Professor Johnson in his contribution to the original *Symposium* never even contemplates the employment and investment effects, but restricts himself to a completely imaginary exercise about once-for-all production and consumption effects based not on the possibility of increasing returns (I agree with his scepticism on that score, as against the puerile optimism of the American sponsors of the Common Market), but on pure comparative cost advantages: he forgets that most of these advantages are the result of historical accidents and if they prevail the weaker countries, i.e. countries weak in the most productive branches, will for ever be precluded from changes.

[2] Perhaps one ought to be thankful that the advice of the officials is usually veiled in secrecy, if only in order that confidence should be retained. At any rate, Sir Edgar Cohen's recent defence of the Free Trade Area proposals (*Board of Trade Journal*, 1958, No. 7, pp. 975–8) betrays a lack of knowledge of elementary economic analysis and a failure to appreciate economic facts which is frightening. He advances ridiculous arguments to defend the exclusion of agriculture from the scheme (p. 977), though he ought to know that it is this field in which the comparative cost differences (and even absolute ones) are really significant. He seems completely ignorant of the likely effects on the less developed or dynamic industries of the competitive blow of stronger ones. There is no hint of alternative policies safeguarding our interests should the British proposals prove unacceptable.

To argue that linking Britain to the latter would have disastrous effects is completely to misunderstand the problem. Even though France before the last devaluation had a highly unfavourable balance of payments, she could not of course have imposed upon Britain her ' price level ' in the sense as it affects the balance of payments.[1] It was not merely that the French prices were high, but that French expenditure on the war plus modernisation was too great relative to production and consumption levels for France to be able to hold a balance in international affairs without severe restrictions at home. The French miracle shows how superficial the problems were (as, of course, were also the British ones in 1957). Once a decision was taken to put the burden of readjustment on the working-class (and this could be enforced because of the change in the political situation), the French balance of payments ' miraculously ' changed, and it is the rest of Europe which is now concerned with the French competitive power. This ' miracle ' shows that the French case that no abolition of tariffs is possible without some harmonisation of policies was essentially right. I feel that Mr. Worswick is wrong in calling the British Free Trade Area proposal ' simple and practical '. It was simple merely in that it proposed to liberalise where Britain had an advantage, and it was never practical because, apart from the threat to which, in my opinion, it would have opened the British market, the—relatively and absolutely—under-developed countries could not possibly have swallowed it.

From this point of view the further British argument that the ' Imperial preferences ' could not be granted to the Free Trade Area countries, because they represent a *quid pro quo*, was profoundly hypocritical. While maintaining them the British representatives wished to obtain equal treatment with the Six in the markets of the Six, without taking the common obligations. It is clear that the French were abundantly justified in not agreeing to the British obtaining equal access to the Common Market in those fields in which they were strongest, without contributing to the maintenance of balance within the community, i.e. liberalising immigration regulations and participating in providing grants for capital development, and adjusting their economic policy, or accepting the same obligations as are forced on the entrepreneurs within the Common Market in the matter of outside tariffs and social charges. The British were told of this (though it does not appear from the papers published) roughly two years ago. They were handed a memorandum which contained the agreed views of the Six over a year ago. They chose to ignore it. Mr. Maudling systematically postponed the discussion of every contentious point in respect to the obligations which, in the view of the Six, were a precondition of their assent to the formation of the Free Trade Area. The inference is obvious that this tactic was to reserve all contentious matter to the end

[1] This was well understood in Germany. The quantitative impact of these differences was analysed in detail (*The Economist*, December 13th, 1958, p. 971).

and then confront the Six with the possibility of a complete break, the abolition of O.E.E.C., and the break-up of E.P.U. This he duly did. Unfortunately he was misinformed about the possibility of breaking the Franco-German *entente*. He then used Monsieur Soustelle's undiplomatically anti-British declaration to break up the negotiations though it contained neither more nor less than what the French had told the British negotiators all along.

The final act of folly was to use the pretext of the French currency and budget ' reform ' to end E.P.U., which the Bank and the Treasury hated as in some way derogatory to the ' status ' of Sterling.[1] With this roughly $1,000m. of internal European liquidity was annihilated. Its successor, the European Monetary Agreement, is a feeble instrument without any automatism. It merely provides for a possible extension of short and medium credit under a dollar guarantee. But the decision is left to the Governments concerned. Thus the possibly adverse consequences of liberalisation on domestic economic policies and growth are no longer (at least partly) buffered or insulated.

The three years that have passed since I wrote my contribution to the *Symposium* have amply confirmed my misgivings about European ' integration ' without safeguards for expansion. Growth practically ceased in Britain for three years, and there is little doubt that fears for the balance of payments were a contributory cause. Even within the Six there has been a (slighter) setback. The Iron and Steel Community has unmasked itself as a cartel and could not deal with the problem of excess coal production *as a unit*. Italian smaller industry has come under pressure. The present recovery does not even represent a catching up with the old trend.

It has also become clear that without powerful help smaller areas, e.g. Austria, would find it difficult to recoup themselves for what they lose in general industry by the expansion of specialised branches.[2] And the political unity of the Western Powers has been weakened by General de Gaulle's and Dr. Adenauer's ambitions and capacity to enforce their views.

II. WITHDRAWAL TO SOMEWHERE

What then is to be the British attitude now?

In my opinion the answer will still depend in the main on the relative weight attached to the political and economic advantages and disadvantages of joining the Common Market in contrast to a retreat towards the Sterling Area.

The British official view now seems to wish to use the Outer Seven

---

[1] E.P.U. was almost wrecked at its inception by the Treasury representatives, and only saved by the direct intervention of Mr. Gaitskell.

[2] This is quite natural. Bavaria, e.g., is on the whole worse off than the more industrialised parts of Austria, though the former is not poorer in national resources than Austria and though Germany as a whole is far stronger and richer than Austria.

as a means, not to force an entry into the Common Market,[1] but, to revive the larger Free Trade Area on the basis of fewer obligations than are now imposed upon the Common Market members but rather more closely co-ordinated than the original Free Trade Area. They feel, and, given the views of Dr. Etzel, who was Dr. Erhard's rival in the recent struggle for succession to Dr. Adenauer, they have some reason to do so, that the threat of exclusion from the markets of the Outer Seven will weigh so heavily with the Germans that, together with their desire for a liberal solution, it will make that vital marginal difference which will encourage the Germans to force their views on the French.

I believe that this attitude is mistaken on two grounds. In the first place the Outer Seven are in no position (apart from Britain and just possibly Sweden) to threaten trade from the Common Market, because they are extremely vulnerable to retaliation by the latter. The visible exports of the remaining five to the Common Market amounted to $1.8 billion in 1957, the imports to $2.4 billion. While this would seem to put the most important members of the Outer Seven (including Britain) in a position to hurt more than they can be hurt, nevertheless if the tourist trade, electricity exports and the like are taken into account, as well as the difficulty of finding alternative markets for iron ore, timber, pulp and certain foodstuffs, the situation is by no means as good as would seem to appear from the global figures.[2] While the timber and paper industries might benefit in Austria, in most of engineering (including electrical) goods the industries can hardly be maintained against free competition of Germany. I feel, therefore, that it is a mistake to assume that the threat of the Seven will be regarded as more than a bluff by the Six.

My second doubt centres round the political needs of Germany and France, which I discussed in the introductory part of this paper. I do not believe that the marginal impact of displacement in the Outer Seven of German exports which is likely, given Germany's dynamism, will be sufficiently serious to induce Germany to change sides and to break the Rome Treaties. It should be remembered that there is no possibility within the Rome Treaties to get round France's veto. In any case success in this venture would merely lead us back to the objection against the original Free Trade Area Scheme.

As all liberalisation schemes, both the Common Market and the Free Trade Area schemes have two main types of impact effect. In the first place they lead to a qualitative change in the pattern of production and consumption, and in the second they influence total demand, investment and employment. The first has been analysed in formal terms as the

---

[1] Cf. Mr. Maudling's speech to the Council of Europe's Consultative Assembly (*The Times*, April 28th, 1959, p. 6).

[2] The Creditanstalt-Bankverein in Vienna made a useful study of how vulnerable a small country is in all except very special industries to the competitive force of larger countries. ('Austria's Relationship to the Larger European Market ', 1959.)

'trade diverting' and 'trade creating' effect. In fact these will be subordinate to the impact on employment and investment, for all 'adjustment' necessitates investment and if a situation is created in which investment is discouraged a net shrinkage of activity might well be the result. It is surprising that this basically Keynesian conclusion has so consistently been disregarded in this field by otherwise most ardent disciples of Keynes. It is probable that this employment effect is positively desired by the more intransigent entrepreneurial circles. They hope that 'free' trade will strengthen their hand against the Trade Unions and are willing to pay the price.[1] Hence the surprising acceptance of the extremely liberal F.T.A. scheme by the F.B.I.

The second of these effects is usually disregarded as being of a temporary character. In my opinion this is illegitimate. A devastating competitive blow to an important industry in any part of the area, while more efficient competititors are expanding elsewhere, will not merely necessitate a once-for-all adjustment but might leave the weaker part of the area absolutely poorer without hope of recouping itself unless very strong measures are taken to boost investment. The uncertainty and risk caused by the existence of strong and powerful competitors within the combined area will reduce investment and thus retard and impede the change in the productive structure which is needed if the weaker area is to recover from and offset the consequences of the blow received.

It is quite illegitimate to assume that the effects of contraction and expansion induced by unification will be *automatically balanced in every single unit of the area*. This was never claimed even by classical economists, and, it is an inference whose validity has been undermined by the vast number of wrecked regions which were cajoled or pressed into political or economic union with stronger partners.

Liberal economists dismiss the effect on employment and the power to obtain readjustment by further investment, and attach great importance to the increase of specialisation and productivity. Here the liberal economists divide into two camps. There are those who believe in increasing returns. They have an easy task. They merely have to show that by combination productivity will increase and great gains will be made, and that these gains will accrue in a random manner over the whole area, i.e. there will be an equalisation of gains and losses with gains predominating.

It was easy for the critics of this case to show that at any rate in the large countries such as Germany or Britain the size of the productive unit was not determined by the size of the market but by oligopolistic imperfections, and that therefore there was little chance of very considerable advances being made. The 'liberals' then fell back on a sort of theological argument which assumed increasing costs all round but nevertheless assumed that by combining an area of competitive industries

[1] The attitude of the Trade Unions is less easily understood.

a gain would accrue, because even though production in the expanding areas would be increasing in cost this increase would be less than the cost in the comparatively less efficient part of the area. The answer to this is twofold. First of all there is no *a priori* reason to believe that in manufactures cost differences are ordained by nature and irremediable. Therefore the weaker country, denied a chance of improving efficiency as a result of the shock effect, will be permanently prevented from increasing its productivity by diversification and investment.

Secondly, and perhaps even more important, the liberalisation, unless it is accompanied by immensely powerful anti-cartel legislation and administration, would result in a vast increase in cartel arrangements and leave the situation much as it was except that the power of determining the location of industry will pass from governments to private interests in which the strongest will increasingly be German dominated.[1] It is inconceivable that any country except perhaps Germany will permit the British to impose such anti-monopoly legislation which would condemn their industries to perdition. And they will be right in as far as any such liberalisation would be detrimental to the poorer areas. What is in fact likely to happen if cartel arrangements do not prevent it, is that new and developing industries in the dynamic countries are likely to displace the less dynamic and less developed ones, lessen employment opportunities and, at least relatively, decreased productivity is likely to be the consequence for the less favoured areas. The less favoured areas in this sense would include areas where trade union strength is strong and social service charges heavy in terms of growth relative to that in other countries. While, therefore, I believe that cartel arrangements are inevitable, I hold that their prevention would have worse consequences. Nevertheless private cartel arrangements are far worse than a democratically controlled system of protection.

In my opinion, therefore, the British Government will have to retreat from its present position and try to obtain new allies in its endeavour to put European trade on a new footing. Such allies can be obtained from among those in the Common Market, and they are powerful, who believe that the safeguards in the Common Market Treaty did not go far enough and who wish to strengthen the European Investment Bank and the harmonisation proposals in the Common Market Treaty. The fact that the Greek and Turkish applications have been favourably considered in the Common Market,[2] while they increase rather than decrease this aspect of the Rome Treaties, shows the power of our potential allies on this new tack. This does not mean that the French are not protectionist and would not like to restrict competition. But it means that from a long-run

---

[1] This in fact has happened both in the case of the Coal and Steel Community and the Common Market.

[2] This contrasts with the apparent decision (taken by the Portuguese Dictatorship on purely prestige grounds) to treat Portugal as a fully developed area by the Outer Seven.

point of view the French conception of the Common Market is potentially constructive. It can, without much difficulty, be squared with the special ties which Britain still has with the Commonwealth and especially the Sterling Area, attenuated as they are by the headlong rush towards convertibility and non-discrimination.

Positive safeguards will be needed to eliminate dangerous tendencies towards the concentration of power and wealth in the new trading area. There would have to be some agreement on the location of industry (possibly through the granting of commercial preference) and a strong agency to provide the financial means. The disparate parts of Europe (and if possible, the Commonwealth and other related areas) must not merely be made more complementary but also more equally productive. Apart from this *long-term* investment programme care would have to be taken to prevent persistent unbalances in the intra-Trading Area payments causing competitive and cumulative deflation.

Any liberalisation scheme necessarily increases the possibility of an unbalance. It also makes it more difficult to restore balance by remedial measures. The volume of trade is increased, therefore any given change in the balance will require a smaller proportional change in exports or imports. But unless automatic finance of deficits is secured or re-established, there will always be reluctance to permit such deficits, especially if there is full convertibility. Thus there will be a definite deflationary bias in the system.[1] Unfortunately the automatic finance of a large portion of the deficits has come to an end through the dissolution of E.P.U. Its speedy restoration is therefore one of the conditions of a successful operation of any European trading system. The restoration of convertibility has made this very much more difficult because extra-group currencies (e.g. dollars) might be demanded and payments are no longer cleared between Central Banks but effected through free markets.[2] A satisfactory technical solution of granting automatic credits is therefore hardly possible: once *universal* convertibility rules, automatic *regional* monetary agreements in the narrowest sense are precluded.[3]

In these circumstances a threefold system of countercyclical and

---

[1] I am interested to see that Professor Triffin now shares this view. Cf. ' Money and Credit ', Review of the *Banca Nazionale di Lavoro*, 1959, pp. 131–200.

[2] A foretaste of the difficulties likely to be encountered has been given by the severe losses of gold suffered as a result of the decision to support ' transferable ' sterling against dollars. Britain's European trading partners had the advantage of being able to obtain 100 per cent in gold without appearing to be persistent creditors: any sales of sterling in Zurich or New York would diminish the credit balance in the subsequent European clearing.

[3] Professor Triffin's European Clearing House (*ibid.*) is not a clearing house at all. It is an attempt to concentrate regional reserves and use them for intra-group lending: it is not likely that the creditor central banks which have acquired such power under the European Monetary agreement will forego these—unless a much more powerful European organ comes into being than now looks probable. Once the regional payments system organised by Governments was destroyed, Central Banks' lending reassumes its importance as an act of grace. The stand-by credits for France were, as in the best days of Montagu Norman, arranged by Central Banks.

long-run equalising safeguards[1] and commercial concessions seems needed. Much the most important of these are (in conditions of convertibility) preferential terms accorded to the exports of the less favoured areas. This has been accepted by the Common Market in respect to the overseas territories of its members (but never contemplated by Britain). Overseas territories can be associated with the Common Market on the basis of ' free ' exports while retaining the right of ' levying tariffs which correspond to the needs of their development and to the requirements of their industrialisation or which, being of a fiscal nature, have the object of contributing to their budget '. This would improve the terms of trade of these countries. The increase in purchasing power is unlikely to be sufficient to narrow the difference in investment capacity enough to ensure equality. Thus further measures will be needed on the financial plane. There will have to be some regard to the payments position of the areas as a whole in relation to the rest of the world because of the *fait accompli* of convertibility. While this latter consideration is at the moment of little importance, the dollar being under pressure, it might revive suddenly should, for instance, the efforts at relaxing cold war tension be successful.[2] The size of U.S. military expenditure and grants is, as already mentioned, more important than the loss of gold. And it is by no means certain that they would be expeditiously replaced by foreign aid for the development of poor countries. Thus at any rate for an intermediate period, in which American public opinion can readjust itself to the need for new obligations, some intra-European defence mechanism shielding the least favourably situated areas in Europe from the impact of further abrupt U.S. changes reversing the present trend of the balance of payments seems needed.

It should be noted that any intra-European investment scheme and the control of industrial location aimed at mitigating and in the end eliminating escapable inequalities, due to lack of capital, skill, or technical knowledge, would *ipso facto* minimise the likelihood of an intra-European unbalance: it is the weaker primary producing countries which are likely to get into balance of payments difficulties.

This has been realised by the French negotiators of the Rome Treaties who were amazingly successful in imparting to what Dr. Erhard wished to reduce to a mere liberalisation scheme (à la F.T.A.), an interventionist-planning bias both in respect to European members and even more to underdeveloped areas. In fact the latter is as complete as might be desired on the commercial side. What needs to be done is a strengthening of the financial safeguards of the Rome Treaties, especially as the differences

---

[1] This system was suggested in a universalist context as early as 1943 (' New Plans for International Trade ' by M. Kalecki, E. F. Schumacher and T. Balogh. Supplement No. 5 to *Bulletin of the Institute of Statistics*, 1943).

[2] Alternatively (and this would be even more tragic) the fear of the unfavourable consequences of disarmament might make people—possibly subconsciously—disinclined for a *détente*.

in economic strength between European countries (as against overseas territories) is not recognised on the *commercial* plane and has to be dealt with entirely on the investment plane.

With German investment running at some $12,000 million as against our $8,500 million, the global resources of the European Investment Bank at some $1,000 million could hardly even make an impression on the problem of intra-European inequality. What would be needed is an *annual* allocation of investment funds for the purpose of at least $500 million and preferably $1,000 million to be financed by contributions which should be fixed by a mechanical formula the basis of which is the income per head, investment per head of the working population, and the annual surplus in the balance of payments. This must be coupled with permission to poor areas to continue their protective measures for at least 20 years with an economic commission to decide whether the time has arrived to permit liberalisation without untoward impact on the poor areas.

Once such an Investment Equalisation Fund has been established, economic discipline will have to be enforced. In other words, care has to be taken that help given to the poorer areas is not wasted on luxury imports or investment and that, even in richer areas with low investment rates, measures are taken to accelerate growth. It is one of the most disappointing features of the activities of the I.M.F. and (to a slightly lesser extent) the I.B.R.D., that they pay exclusive attention to what they call ' equilibrium ' in the *monetary system and balance of payments*. This can be achieved either by *speedy development* creating new export markets, or displacing imports, or by *curbing investment and income*. The latter method in present political conditions inevitably results in the recurrence of ' inflation ' as no government (not excluding dictatorial ones) can possibly afford discontent inescapable if stagnation continues unbroken. Thus in a less progressive economy there will be periodic crises resulting from attempts to increase consumption out of proportion to the restricted possibilities due to low investment. The British, French, Spanish and Turkish examples should suffice. The deflationist method does not yield economic balance compatible with social stability. If discipline, in the sense of taking energetic measures to increase investment, is secured a forward-looking method of maintaining balance in international payments will at last have been developed which assures balance but reduces international inequality.

Temporary unbalance could be dealt with by an automatic increase in the resources made available to the Agency by countries unduly gaining reserves in the form of medium-term loans, to be extended if the creditor position persists. The increased contribution could be fixed as an increasing percentage of the gain in gold reserves by the creditor country. Thus temporary, cyclical unbalances could also be used for the basic aim of accelerating and equalising investment.

It is obvious that no such commitments could be undertaken by Britain unless Commonwealth co-operation can be secured and unless certain other vitally important areas, e.g. of the Middle East, could get access to the new organisation. Otherwise the discrimination in Europe in favour of certain overseas territories and independent countries might seriously injure other, not less poor and not less deserving areas.

So far as the undeveloped areas of the Commonwealth are concerned the problem is comparatively simple. The overseas territories of France, Belgium and Holland have received exceptionally favoured treatment in as much as their produce can be exported duty free to the Common Market while they develop their industries. In the case of the highly developed Commonwealth countries the problem is very much more difficult. Canada in particular, being a member of the Dollar Area, represents a formidable complication.

Two alternatives are open. Either imperial preference can be harmonised and extended without more ado to the members of the Common Market, or a two-tier preference system can be adopted similar to the Carli plan. Both would however necessitate American consent because of the unfortunate G.A.T.T. obligation.

The two-tier preference system could be either (a) a basically free trade area, where countervailing duties are only imposed on food and raw materials in which the tariffs of the members to third countries differ, and which have no duties against one another, or (b) a double preferential system in a narrower sense where each of the members has duties against the other but they are lower than those against third countries.

The highly developed independent members of the Sterling Area are unlikely to opt for anything more than (b). In that case, our preferences in the Commonwealth would remain above the preferences granted to the Six or the Seven and special treatment in respect of foodstuffs could be assured to the former.

All this suggests that it would be essential to obtain a much closer agreement on policy with the Sterling Area countries before attempting to go much further either with the Outer Seven or the Six. A Commonwealth Investment Fund, for instance, might be the nucleus of a wider organisation of Western Europe and its related territories abroad. This is far more important than the present effort at forming an undefined and hardly definable arrangement with the Outer Seven which hardly take a tenth of our exports (though they absorb a higher portion of the Common Market exports than the Sterling Area).

If no Commonwealth agreement could be obtained to our participation in a closer European Trade Organisation, the next best solution would be the re-creation of a closely co-ordinated and actively functioning Sterling Area. Even this might now prove impossible—though I believe it ought to be tried. Only if it failed would I think of severing the remaining ties of the Sterling Area—coming to some agreement about Sterling balances—and try entry into a European Trade Organisation without the Commonwealth. The least palatable solution would be ' to go it alone ' or merely with the Outer Seven.

In all these cases, however, a drastic increase in British domestic investment and foreign lending capacity is the necessary (if not sufficient) condition of a successful solution.

The comparative indicators of economic growth show our inferiority in Europe. This inferiority is still increasing. It is far greater in relation to the Communist countries. We cannot rely on the latter continuing to abstain from mutually profitable trade. If they do not, our terms of trade suffer and with it our capacity to maintain balance without having to cut living standards, or at least stagnate.

Unfortunately there seems very little realisation of the dangers and opportunities facing Britain. And official policy seems frozen in the posture which has been responsible for our present weakness which is masked by a number of exceptional but transitory factors.

THE COMMON MARKET: THE ECONOMISTS' REACTIONS

By HARRY G. JOHNSON

I. POSTSCRIPT[1]

My main contribution to the second round of this symposium is the estimate of the value of the Free Trade Area to Britain, which was originally published in the *Manchester School*. I am extremely grateful to the editor of this volume for allowing it to be included, both because it may help to dispel any impression created by my first-round comments that I was ungenerously expecting Mr. Black to do all the work,[2] and because it illustrates, in a very rudimentary form, the kind of exercise that needs to be undertaken if economists are to play a professionally, and not merely a ceremonially, adequate role in the formation of economic policy. The calculation is, of course, very rough; the Economist Intelligence Unit's figures are incomplete, the method by which they were obtained not altogether clear, and the partisan tone of the volume in which they were

[1] The general reader is advised to proceed to the next section of this piece, which is more entertaining.

[2] I still think it was fair to comment that the facts which Mr. Black had assembled and presented as relevant to discussion of the issues were of little use in assessing the economic gains and losses indicated by theoretical analysis. Selection of such facts for presentation presumably implies motivation by some criterion of relevance, even if interpretation of the facts is left to others.

published not altogether reassuring. Moreover, the calculation refers to only one aspect of the difference between the effects of Common Market alone and Common Market *cum* Free Trade Area: insofar as economies of scale, the growth-and-efficiency-stimulating effects of competition, the terms-of-trade effects of discrimination, and so forth are meaningful arguments, they too demand an attempt at quantification. Nevertheless, publication of even such a minimal effort at quantification seems justified by the light it throws on the order of magnitude of the gains from improved specialisation and division of labour that might result from establishment of a free trade area, especially in view of the paucity of calculations of the effects of commercial policy in the literature of international trade.[1]

Though the calculation is so rough and ready, it can fairly plausibly be predicted that a more refined calculation would yield a measure of gain of a similar order of magnitude, namely something under five per cent of national income.[2] This is because the gains result from the substitution of a lower-cost for a higher-cost source of supply for the satisfaction of wants (and conversely for losses). On the one hand, the degree of substitutability between different goods and between similar goods from different sources may, on the basis of evidence of various kinds, be assumed in general to be low.[3] On the other, differences in costs attributable to deliberate acts of commercial policy are likely to be small in proportionate terms, or to apply to goods relatively unimportant in total consumption, simply because there are limits to the amount of damage from protection that consumers will put up with. Thus both elements in the calculation are likely to be small, in relation to the price and quantity components of national income, and their product consequently even smaller in relation to national income.[4]

This does not necessarily imply that the potential gains from freer

---

[1] Only two serious efforts to quantify the effects of a country's tariff have been published: that of the committee of four economists on the effects of the Australian tariff—the Brigden Committee—of 1929, and the study by Dr. J. H. Young contained in his *Canadian Commercial Policy*, prepared for the Royal Commission on Canada's Economic Prospects and published in 1958.

[2] Tibor Scitovsky, in his *Economic Theory and Western European Integration*, using P. J. Verdoorn's econometric estimates of the effects of European Integration and a method identical with mine, calculates the gain from increased specialisation at 'less than one-twentieth of one per cent of the gross social product of the countries involved' (p. 67)—a result of an even smaller order of magnitude than my own.

[3] Considering the economic chaos that would result from chance movements in prices and exchange rates if substitutability between goods were high, one is led to the conclusion either that general jointness of demand is a fortunate accident which has permitted the survival of capitalism, or that the production of goods differentiated to some degree from one another is a consequence of the stability requirements of a competitive system.

[4] Assume that imports can be treated as a single commodity subject to a uniform tariff rate. Then the gain from adopting free trade (apart from economies of scale and terms of trade effects) defined on Marshallian surplus lines and measured as a proportion of national expenditure at market prices, is $\frac{1}{2}\tau^2\eta\nu$, where τ is the proportion of the tariff in the market price of imports, η the elasticity of import demand, and ν the proportion of expenditure on imports in national expenditure at market prices. On the very generous assumptions of $\tau = \frac{1}{4}$ (i.e. a tariff rate of $33\frac{1}{3}$ per cent), and $\nu = \frac{1}{4}$, η would have to exceed 6.4 for the gain to exceed 5 per cent of national income.

trade are negligible—most things over which economic policy has control, other than the level of effective demand, probably have a small influence on potential national income at any one time. Even if the gains from improved specialisation and division of labour are regarded as marginal, the effects of greater freedom of trade on economic welfare may still (*pace* Balogh, Kahn and Worswick) be important, because its effects on the rate of adoption of innovations and on the rate of investment, whatever their direction, may be more important than its effects on resource allocation.[1]

II. RETROSPECT

The estimate of the value of the Free Trade Area was made when the negotiations to associate a Free Trade Area with the Common Market still looked like coming to a successful conclusion. Those negotiations have since failed and the Government has instead taken a lead in establishing a smaller Free Trade Area in rivalry to the Common Market. Rather than pursue further the problem of measuring the potential gains from a Free Trade Area on the original lines, or attempt an adaptation of the method to the new prospective system of European trade, I think it interesting at this stage to look backward, in a critical fashion, to the climate of opinion among British economists at the state of negotiations corresponding roughly to the first round of the symposium, because the initial reactions of economists to the Free Trade Area scheme seem to me to reveal certain weaknesses of general approach to policy problems of this nature which should not pass unnoticed.

Generalization about states of opinion is notoriously dangerous; but it seems a fairly justifiable observation that the Free Trade Area scheme developed so rapidly that most of the profession were caught unprepared, and consequently tended both to form their opinions on it in the light of not-altogether-relevant habitual attitudes and to evaluate its economic effects by means of rule-of-thumb methods of doubtful economic value, with the result that the collective literature on the subject leaves something to be desired as evidence of professional expertise. It is even possible that unpreparedness and insufficiently cautious expression of opinion on the part of the general body of economists contributed something to the eventual failure of the Government's negotiations with the Six, in that by-and-large economists accepted, or at least did not actively challenge, both the Government's offensively Anglo-centric definition of the problem as one of obtaining the maximum gains from freer trade with Europe at the minimum sacrifice of other British interests, and its vulnerable belief

---

[1] The view expressed in Worswick's second contribution, that freedom of trade merely magnifies the effects of expansionary or deflationary forces originating autonomously in countries' internal economic development seems to me far too simplified. Much of the argument both for and against freedom of trade is concerned with its influence on the rate of economic growth, a subject on which there seems to be no clear-cut empirical evidence.

F

that Britain stood to lose a great deal economically from establishment of a Common Market without a surrounding Free Trade Area.

A re-reading of the first round of this symposium leaves me with a strong impression that the contributions were both predictable, and predictably unsatisfying as a guide to the economics of the policy problem. A maliciously hostile critic might even go so far as to summarize the symposium in the following terms: Mr. Black, perhaps from a desire to avoid the chastisement with whips and scorpions customarily inflicted on the lead writers in *Bulletin* symposia by the other contributors, confined himself to the assembly of facts so arid that no-one else tried seriously to use them; Professor Johnson took a high theoretical line and demanded an impossible calculation, which he carefully refrained from making himself, though he did not refrain from making fairly definite casual suggestions as to what the answer would be; Dr. Balogh, his emotions as usual more obvious than his conclusions, produced his familiar complicated problem play, with Germany instead of the United States this time appearing as the villain of the piece; Mr. Harrod surveyed the field with sturdy Christ Church Common Room common sense, displaying a remarkably confident intuitive knowledge of the economics of motor car production; Mr. Sargent kept his eyes firmly fixed on the peripheral problem of stock fluctuations and his own solution of temporary quantitative restrictions; Professor Kahn began with an introspective tour of an unusually subtle psyche and ended by reiterating his well-known discovery that a regional bloc can obtain terms-of-trade benefits from discrimination against the outside world[1]; and Mr. Worswick, in his privileged position of herald to the tournament, demonstrated the weak spots in his contributors' armour with point, blade, or flat of his sword as the occasion offered, without engaging anyone in actual combat.

Such an account would, of course, be caricature of the most exaggerated, unfair, and possibly libellous sort; but it would contain some grain of truth, in that all contributors, faced with the problem of evaluating a scheme whose effects would be far-reaching changes in economic structure of a sort easy enough to predict in direction but extremely difficult to predict in magnitude, were under a strong inducement either to exaggerate the relevance of the knowledge they were sure of, or to form and use judgments as to the magnitudes of various economic effects based necessarily on one degree or another of sheer speculation. In this respect the contributors were in no different a position than the general body of British economists, faced with an urgent policy problem on which an economist would naturally be expected to have some sort of opinion; and it seems fairer to discuss the reactions of economists as a group in general terms,

---

[1] So delighted was he with this thought that he apparently forgot that in the Viner analysis trade diversion is a cause of loss, not gain; in fact the region gains on its terms of trade to the extent that trade diversion does *not* take place.

rather than to concentrate on the particular selection of individuals participating in the symposium.

The most striking characteristic of the reactions of British economists to the Common Market and Free Trade Area schemes, viewed in the light of subsequent developments, was the solidary Britishness they displayed. With few exceptions, if any, the economists seem to have agreed with the Government's general line both that freedom of trade, and not freedom of factor movements or the co-ordination of economic policies and institutions, is the substance of economic co-operation, and that what had to be decided was the terms on which Britain would be willing to join with the Six. None, so far as I can recall, showed any very profound appreciation of the possibility that the Six might have quite a different conception of economic co-operation than the British, let alone any sympathy with this conception or willingness to consider its merits as against trade-orientated British conceptions. It has since become clear enough that the Six, or at least the French, do take their alternative conception of economic co-operation seriously. But recognition of this fact has tended to be more a matter of growing irritation with French perversity than of British self-questioning; while the fact that Britain has been trying to muscle in on a scheme whose earlier development she had formerly been steadily resisting, has been conveniently forgotten. The celebrated *Times* headline, ' France the Wrecker ', epitomizes this attitude; a headline more in accord with the historical evolution of events might well have been ' Britain the Uninvited Guest '.

The insularity of the reactions of British economists, and the grudgingness with which they tend to recognize the Continental viewpoint, is reflected (*inter alia*) in some passages of Mr. Worswick's account of the negotiations. Thus Mr. Worswick finds in statements of the aims of the Rome Treaty ' a strain of almost mystical fervour . . . uncongenial to British statesmen, administrators and economists ' whose existence should nevertheless have been recognized ' as a factor in the situation '—in blunter words, the desire to create a unified economy is not a reasonable policy objective, but a delusion whose possessor should be treated with due gentleness. (How, incidentally, a country in which so much play can be made with concepts like ' the strength of sterling '. ' Commonwealth ties ', and ' colonial responsibilities ' can affect to despise other countries' strains of mystical fervour is hard to understand.) Again, in discussing the alternatives for Britain, Mr. Worswick concedes something to the Six, *insofar as* what they were opposing might have been ' a doctrinaire adherence to free trade as such ' on the British side, and he raises the question whether the negotiations could have been brought to a successful conclusion if the British had emphasized ' the need for institutions and the co-ordination of policies of *expansion* '—almost as if the Continent was peopled with Labour party sympathizers. Even more revealing, perhaps, of the failure to take much trouble to understand the Continental viewpoint was a personal comment on the failure of the negotiations made to me by an economist[1] who had taken an active part in the debate: 'A great opportunity for giving a lead was lost'. The presumption that Britain gives the lead, and not the support, in relations with the Continent is one of the less attractive myths of British international relations.

On the face of things, the British approach to international economic co-operation through freer trade, supplemented according to taste by measures to ease balance-of-payments problems and to maintain high employment, is by no means self-evidently the only sensible one. Though the free-trade tradition dominates the development of modern Anglo-Saxon economics, there is a not entirely unrespectable tradition favouring the protected (and integrated) market as the instrument of economic welfare; and though much of the Continental argument about the necessity of harmonization of wages, social conditions, *etcetera* to secure the benefits of specialization and division of labour is demonstrable nonsense, there may be a broader environmental sense in which harmonization of institutions fosters efficiency and growth. More cogent than these possibilities is the consideration that freedom of movement of factors of production, envisaged in the Common Market but not in the Free Trade Area, may be a far more important means of securing both efficient use of resources and the stimulation of growth than mere freedom of movement of commodities. It is only too easily forgotten that freedom of movement of labour and capital, as well as of goods, was a characteristic of the nineteenth century.[2]

The foregoing remarks pertain to the narrowly Anglo-centric way in which the majority of British economists conceived of economic co-operation with the Common Market countries. It is also possible to discern certain common characteristics in the way in which the economic effects of the Free Trade Area scheme tended to be assessed, characteristics which cannot be considered as altogether helpful to reasoned assessment of these effects. Two such characteristics are particularly noteworthy; the tendency to use descriptive statistics as if they were arguments, and the use of what may be described as Gestalt, analogue, and psychic methods of arriving at quantitative appraisals of economic significance.

By the tendency to use descriptive statistics as if they were arguments, I refer to the presentation of comparative totals of monetary and physical

---

[1] I refrain from mentioning his name, so that only his closest friends and enemies will recognize him.

[2] One of the striking paradoxes of twentieth-century ' liberal ' international economic policy is that it accepts the imposition of barriers to the movement of labour that wants to move to advanced countries, and in compensation advocates the forced movement of capital that does not want to move to underdeveloped countries. The position of progressive British opinion, which opposes the imposition of barriers to Commonwealth and colonial immigration but would apparently prefer to bribe Italians and other Europeans to stay at home (where they provide a picturesque background for summer holidays) is peculiarly anomalous.

magnitudes, and of percentage breakdowns of totals and indexes of magnitudes over time, in such a way as to imply that they have significance in themselves. A great deal of the literature about the Free Trade Area has consisted of compilations of the total production of this and that that will be included in the Area, the shares of trade in this and that that members do with each other and the outside world, comparative rates of growth of this and that in different countries, and so forth—information which is of no meaning whatsoever, in the context of a problem of this kind, unless accompanied by some analysis of the magnitude and significance of the changes that would result in for example, costs of production or import and export prices or rates of growth, if existing barriers to intra-area trade were removed. It is, unfortunately, only too easy to stop with the statistic, pacified with percentages, thereby thoroughly confusing existing structure with potential structural change; and to imply that anything which is twenty per cent of something else is twice as important as anything which is only ten per cent of it, or that anything which only grew by five per cent during a period when everything else grew by ten per cent was putting up a pretty poor show. Even Mr. Black, who is generally careful to present his statistics without economic interpretation, strays from the path of rectitude to the extent of describing Britain as ' lagging behind the rest of Europe ' on the basis of four indices which show a less rapid rate of growth in Britain than elsewhere since 1953.[1] The plain truth is that facts are only facts; for predicting the effects of economic changes, they cannot take the place of relationships between economic variables: and for evaluating economic performance, they cannot be their own criteria.

By the use of Gestalt, analogue, and psychic methods of arriving at quantitative appraisals of economic significance, I refer to methods which justify a judgment as to the magnitude of a complex change to oneself without necessarily justifying, or even explaining, it to anyone else. The adjectives distinguish methods of achieving this result which differ recognizably, but too subtly to be worth defining closely. Examples of such methods are easily identifiable in the arguments of contributors to the symposium. The most dramatic example of the analogue method is Mr. Harrod's ability, simply by ' having the United States in mind,' to arrive at the conclusion that ' at the most, Britain should not be producing more than one type of car '. Professor Kahn's view that ' in the European context, it is easy to exaggerate the importance of the economies of division of labour and of specialisation, of the spur to efficiency provided by extra competition and of the erosion of profit margins ' appears Gestaltist but turns out on closer inspection to be psychic; while Dr. Balogh's psychic dismissal of economies of scale—' I wonder, however, whether the merely negative act of opening national markets will be sufficient '—is supported

---

[1] To the best of my knowledge, no statistician has ever interpreted such figures to mean that Britain was dawdling in front of the rest of Europe.

by elements of analogue argument. Lest I be thought to be over-indulging in calling kettles black, I should admit at this point that my own argument on economies of scale, which was intended as a criticism of analogue arguments of the Harrod type, and to be based on relating unexploited economies to size of market, is given a definite psychic slant by my use of the phrase, ' it is extremely difficult to believe that . . . ';[1] Mr. Worswick's counter-argument ' but the removal of tariffs must surely have *some* effect in assisting mass production ' is clearly Gestalt.[2]

In criticising the use of these methods of arriving at judgments of economic significance, I should make it clear that I am not objecting to the procedure of guessing at economic magnitudes as such. Given the present and prospective state of knowledge about economic relationships, the labour required for economic calculation, and the fact that the most important decision problems are unique experiments, it is inevitable that economic policy-makers and commentators must rely to a large extent on guessing at the magnitudes of economic effects. What is objectionable is guesswork which produces a final conclusion without either reducing the area within which guesswork is necessary as far as possible, or defining as clearly as possible the nature of the guess and the factors considered in making it. Such guesswork has the undesirable effect of implying that one man's guess is as good as another's, and that there is no great need to try to reduce the area of ignorance.

---

[1] Several people have pointed out to me that the argument is defective on its own grounds, insofar as what matters to the industry is the size of its particular market in the country, which may be small even if the national economy is large, and the formation of a free trade area may merge small national markets into a significantly larger regional market; this sort of result could be quantitatively important in the aggregate.

[2] It also misses the point, since I was not denying that there would be some effects, only arguing that they would be unlikely to be very important.